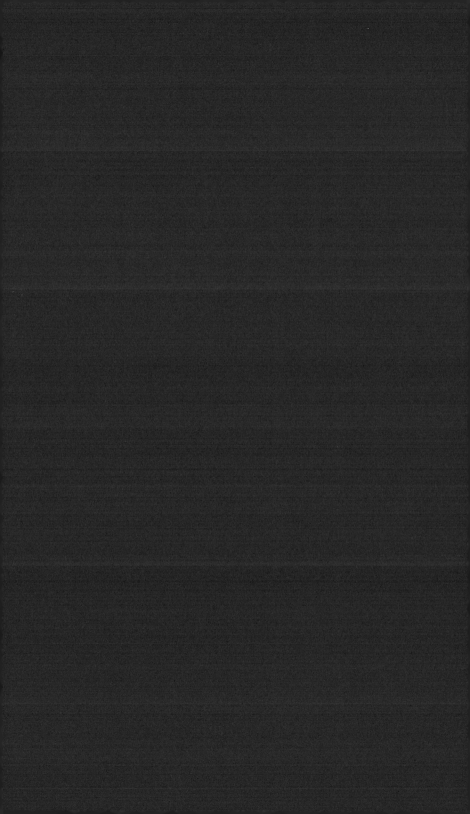

SHEPHERDS
AND THEIR
DOGS

SHEPHERDS
AND THEIR
DOGS

John Bezzant

Merlin Unwin Books

First published in Great Britain by Merlin Unwin Books, 2011

Merlin Unwin Books Ltd
Palmers House
7 Corve Street
Ludlow, Shropshire SY8 1DB
U.K.

www.merlinunwin.co.uk

A CIP catalogue record for this book is available from the British Library.

ISBN 978 1906122 37 9

Designed and set in Bembo by Merlin Unwin
Printed and bound by Jellyfish Print Solutions

CHAPTER ONE

The Partnership

THIS IS a glimpse into the fascinating world of the shepherd and his dogs. An onlooker is often entranced to see a Collie dog sent from his master's side with a single word of command, disappearing with speed and grace up a rock-peppered hillside, reaching the crest in minutes and vanishing over the other side of the hill where it must operate alone, out of the shepherd's sight and out of range of any command. The waiting shepherd leans on his stick in calm contemplation, appearing to the bystander to be a natural part of the landscape, as much part of the scenery as the purple-flowered heather that clothes the hillside with splendour.

At last, a single sheep appears on the crest of the hill, then another and another, till a line of sheep a hundred or more in number are bounding like a stream in winter down the rough hillside. The shepherd watches but does not move and when his dog finally appears, moments after the last sheep has crested the hill, he does not interfere by sending out commands that are not needed. Soon the sheep are before the shepherd in a tight bunch, held together by the dog that mills back and forth, daring them to break rank.

The passerby asks himself what alchemy has taken place, that the dog can be controlled at such distance and out of sight of his master. But there is no magic involved. This great feat is something far more fascinating and commendable: a partnership. On one side there is complete trust and on the other side, absolute devotion. And though not many shepherds would admit it, this is a relationship based on love, the fruits of which are trust and devotion which bind the shepherd and his dog into this complete understanding.

TV programmes and many books expound the theory that a dog only works for his master through the natural instincts of the pack animal, responding to its leader in return for a warm bed and plenty of food. I have never held this point of view. I hope that, as you read the stories that follow, you too will come to the conclusion that there is more to it than that.

★★★★★

So let us begin with a simple demonstration of the shepherd's trust in his four-legged friend, taken from the late 1800s. There are no names in this account because the shepherd involved was by no means unique: what he did was common to all shepherds. This shepherd had grazing for his flock some three miles down the road from the farm. The route from farm to grazing was full of twists and turns with many gates and steep banks. Rather than make the time-consuming six mile round trip each day, the shepherd left the task of taking the flock to the grazing to his Collie dog.

Each morning, in response to a single command, the dog took the sheep the three miles to the pasture, staying with the flock the entire day to ensure that they did not cross the boundaries of the shepherd's land. The dog knew these limits exactly and he would also protect the sheep from any dangers, whether thieves or stray dogs. Then at exactly the same hour before dusk every day, the dog would quietly gather up his charges and return them to the farm. Such trust was commonplace between shepherds and their dogs during the 1800s and early 1900s and many similar accounts are well documented. The shepherds gave their dogs the kind of responsibility you would give to another human being, such was their confidence in their dogs' intelligence and devotion.

This devotion would take the dog to the brink of death for his master if required, and such was the case on the day that a sheepdog named old Rasp had to take to the water to save a drowning sheep. As this particular shepherd was returning from a day on the hill with his three dogs, old Rasp among them, he was told by neighbours that one of his sheep, a blind creature that usually stayed close to the farm, had fallen into the loch and was surely drowning.

The shepherd with his three dogs at heel rushed down to the lochside to see the poor sheep floundering frantically in an effort to save herself. But with no sight she could not orientate herself to the shore and was rapidly becoming exhausted. If something was not done within the next few minutes, the sheep would drown.

The shepherd knew instinctively that this was a task for his eldest and most experienced dog, the little Rasp. With one word, barely more than a whisper, the command was given and Rasp without a moment's hesitation plunged into the water to save the beleaguered ewe, whose sodden fleece was dragging her down like a lead jacket. Barking and pushing with her nose, Rasp tried to steer the ewe to safety first from one direction then another but try as she might, Rasp could not put the ewe, overcome by fear and exhaustion, onto the right track. Still the little dog would not give up: the command had been issued and she would rather drown herself than give up. The shepherd who knew only too well the devotion of this little dog, began to look concerned, fearing that he was going to lose one of his best friends and most trusted colleagues.

'That ewe is going to drown your dog,' said a concerned bystander.

'Yes,' replied the stern-faced shepherd in a sombre tone, 'She will either die herself or save the sheep.'

After several desperate minutes which seemed to last

To work sheep in wild hill country like this without the partner-
ship of loyal dogs is impossible, as this young shepherdess (Patience
Bissett) well knows.

for hours, the little dog's gargantuan efforts paid off as the
half-drowned ewe finally struggled ashore, followed by old
Rasp, who collapsed exhausted and shivering in the shallows
as she came towards the shore. The shepherd scooped up the
magnificent dog in his arms and carried her to his fireside
where his wife quickly brought the dog round. With devotion
like this, it is not surprising that shepherds were willing to
trust their entire livelihood to their own sheepdogs.

★★★★★

One dark night in the 1800s, a Collie named Sirrah saved
not only his master's livelihood but his reputation and his
pride as well. The shepherd was James Hogg, also known as
the Ettrick Shepherd, Scottish author and shepherd born in

The sheepdog, whatever his breed, will accomplish the given task or die trying to complete it.

1770, who taught himself to read and write and became a published poet. He, with the help of a young lad and Sirrah, had been given the charge over 700 very valuable lambs at weaning time. The lambs were kept at the foot of a hill.

As Mr Hogg and the young lad sat around a glowing fire watching their charges, everything was quiet and relaxed, the gentle bleat of young lambs filling the air with music. Then for no reason whatsoever, the lambs bolted. By the light of the fire the shepherd watched in horror as the huge flock, as if chased by the very devil himself, split into three groups and charged away in different directions before he could raise himself from his seat.

Mr Hogg had never seen the like of it in all his years working as a shepherd: suddenly the entire flock of 700 new lambs were gone - lost in a hundred miles of treacherous hill country. How would he explain to his master that he had lost every last lamb? The master would be furious and Mr Hogg realised he could well lose his job and with it the tied cottage that came with it, he and his family could be without income, without accommodation, and his reputation would be destroyed. Who would ever employ him again - the shepherd who had lost his *entire* flock of lambs! With such desperate thoughts racing like poison through his mind, he spoke quietly to his dog.

'Sirrah, my man,' he said, 'they are away.'

Sirrah understood and read the desperation in his master's voice. Nothing more needed to be said: the dog knew what must be done and set out across the dark hills to save his master from ruin. Mr Hogg admired the spirit of his dog but pondered what one dog could do, faced with such a task: 700 lambs scattered in three flocks in a hundred miles of hill country! It would take a team of shepherds and their dogs a week or two to recover the situation. It was hopeless.

Mr Hogg decided, however, that anything was better than sitting worrying, so he set off into the hills with the young lad, their lanterns little specks of light moving up the black hill. For six and a half hours they tramped the treacherous slopes, never pausing for a rest, but they found nothing:

not even the slightest track or trail. It was as though the hills had opened up and swallowed the lambs forever.

Cold, wet with the morning dew and exhausted, the pair began their descent from the hilltops as the first rays of sunshine crept over a distant mountain range. Mr Hogg knew he now had to return to the farm and tell his master that the lambs were all gone. He was no coward but this task filled him with dread.

However, as he turned back, Mr Hogg spotted with great relief one of the flocks of lambs, some way down the hill in a deep ravine. He rubbed his eyes hard to make sure that the cold, hunger and fatigue were not making him see things – but when he looked again, the lambs were still there and the lad confirmed it with a yelp of excitement. Hurriedly the two made their way down the steep hill, reinvigorated by the find of at least a few of their lambs. It was some consolation. Nearing the mouth of the ravine, Mr Hogg suddenly stopped: these lambs were not simply sheltering as he had first thought. There was Sirrah sitting domineeringly in front of them, holding the lambs in place with his determined eye alone, daring them to try and pass him.

'What a dog,' thought Mr Hogg to himself. As he drew closer, it dawned on him with astonishment that this was not just one of the three flocks that had disappeared into the darkness, but all 700 lambs: not a single one was missing or even injured in any way. How on earth had one dog gathered together three flocks of skittish lambs into one great flock, in total darkness, then driven them to what was in effect a holding pen carved in the land by nature's hand?

The intelligence, the stamina and the skill required to accomplish a task which would have tested a shepherd and three or four Collies to breaking point, was phenomenal, rightly earning Sirrah a place in shepherd's folklore. What had driven faithful Sirrah to push himself to the brink of his abilities? The devoted dog, sensing the anguish in his master's voice, was determined to do all in his power to help his master and that is just what he did. Mr Hogg later stated that he had never felt so grateful to any man on earth as he did to his Sirrah that morning.

It is only when man and dog become one that the dog can feel his masters needs and act to save the day. That one-ness comes about by quiet times spent watching the flock together.

These remarkable accounts illustrate the incredible bond that exists between a true shepherd and his dogs, but how is this relationship brought about? Is it magic, is it method or is it understanding? The following comments from shepherds, recorded in the early part of the 1900s, give us an insight into the training methods of the true shepherd and the guiding principal behind his approach.

'When he is a pup, we teach him to obey his master's call at once. It must be done with kindness or the dog won't love you as he must if he is to serve you well.'

Take note of the words 'love' and 'kindness' for they are the core around which the shepherd builds the entire relationship with his dog.

The maxim of one Scottish shepherd was;

'Make a dog love you and he will never fail or forsake you.'

John Herries McCulloch writes in his splendid little book, *Sheep Dogs And Their Masters*:

'The expert shepherd today works through gentleness, patience and firmness. I do not know one who handles his dogs with harsh severity; I would not care to know such a man.'

It is this ability of the shepherd to mix gentleness and firmness in a perfect balance that wins over a dog. How often among dog owners do we see just one of these qualities? Too much gentleness turns the dog into a bully that rules the roost, and such a dog does not respect its master. Too much firmness breaks a dog's spirit, making it a shadow of what it could be. Such a broken-spirited dog cannot love its master. The shepherd knows that both gentleness and firmness must be measured out, but in varying amounts according to the dog: with one dog a single harsh word once in its lifetime is sufficient to keep it in its correct place; with another dog a constant reminder is in order.

The shepherd raised around sheepdogs knows after spending only a few moments with a dog what measure of gentleness and what measure of firmness it requires to earn its respect and devotion.

As Alexander Millar of Ayrshire said,

'There must be an understanding and sympathy between dog and man.'

And Alexander knew what he was talking about. He won the championship shield at the international sheep dog trial held in Criccieth in 1925 with a dog called Spot, and with the same dog he also won the Scottish national championship three times. His belief was that a man without understanding is blind to the needs of his dog; and a man without sympathy is unable to feel the spirit of his dog.

Mark Hayton, who won the international sheepdog trials in 1926 with his dog Glen said:

'Study nature and encourage nature to improve upon itself. Be infinitely patient; do not offend your dog; do not be easily offended by him. Some dogs can bear much correction. Some are sensitive and can bear little. Study both. If a dog slips off home, find out what caused him to leave you. Avoid corporal punishment.'

In this briefest of statements Mr Hayton encapsulates the essence of dog training: whether for training a sheepdog to work on the hills, a guard dog to protect property or a family pet to have good manners. Study the dog to see what he is, then build upon it. Mr Hayton is telling us to let a dog be itself. Do not force it into a mould of your making but encourage it to be what it is meant to be: respect your dog, he implies, and it will respect you. Notice how he uses the words 'encourage' and 'infinitely patient', for this is where most people go wrong. They try and force a dog to improve with impatience and of course fail.

The shepherd is a watcher, a deep thinker and a well of patience. These are the tools he uses to gain an insight into a dog's soul; the foundation on which the training and the relationship are built.

Welsh Collies with their pipe-smoking master.

Behavioural science related to dogs is very popular these days but the shepherd, without the need for a university degree, has been practising canine behavioural science quietly for hundreds of years, by studying the nature of a dog to find out what he needs and what he can give.

In the pages of this book you will learn much about the relationship that exists between a shepherd and his dogs. Whilst it is entertaining to read about such things, there is also much to be learned and applied to training our own dogs, to make our relationship with them deeper and their lives healthier and happier. If we learn from the shepherd, perhaps we will be able to talk about our dogs as Mr Hayton did when he said of his high-spirited working Collie, 'He clings to his freedom and will not do what he believes to be wrong but his honest heart is still his master's, for whom he lives, breathes and fights.'

CHAPTER TWO

The Nature of the Shepherd

WHAT IS A SHEPHERD? He could be someone in the employ of a great landowner, such as the laird of a Scottish estate. In this case, they would usually be paid by the landowner and live in a tied cottage. Some shepherds are self-employed and work as tenant farmers. There are even travelling shepherds who moved from farm to farm, freelancing where they were required. Most shepherds are of modest means but that is not a prerequisite.

The shepherd of the nineteenth century was known for his quiet, religious, courageous nature. When not out on the hills, and fields – which was most of the time – the centre of his home-life would be the kitchen, warmed by a peat fire in many parts of the country, with white-washed walls often hung with the fleeces of sheep found dead on the mountain. The focus of the room would be the dining table, surrounded by benches. Most shepherds would allow their sheepdogs to sleep in the gloomy kitchen, with small dusty windows and the door often kept ajar to allow more light in. Braxy hams (dried and salted mutton hams) would hang from the ceiling; and by the fire, depending on the part of the country, strings of fish. In the window of each shepherd's house would, traditionally, be a candle, whose beam has saved many a shepherd's life, as a beacon directing the way to home from the dark or snowy hillsides.

The calling of shepherd tended to be passed from one generation directly to the next: in Sussex in 1850, one line of shepherds could trace their roots in that way of life back for two hundred years. The advantage of the job passing from father to sons and daughters was that there would be an accumulation of skill ingrained from birth. Women were shepherdesses in the same way as the men.

The shepherd's children, born with the sound of bleating lambs in their ears, would be expected to help on the hillside or in the lambing yard as soon as they were physically able, learning by practical experience and example, taught by their father in the same way that their grandfather will have taught him. As the shepherd's children grew up, they would gradually take on the yoke of responsibility, as the very elderly shepherd grew unable to continue and was able to pass on the role.

Until recent times, shepherds from the South Downs to the north of Scotland had a love of the bible, and when affordable printing allowed it, they carried a pocket version which they would read while watching over their grazing sheep. Not surprisingly, their favourite verses were to be found in the book of Psalms, many of which are written by that most famous of shepherds, David, who as a boy became adept with his sling to protect his flock from wolf and lion and was later to use these shepherding skills against the giant Goliath!

If shepherds were to have their own anthem, it would surely be Psalm 23, here taken from the King James Bible, which is considered by many to be the most beautiful piece of literature ever written and is the version of the Bible the shepherds for the last 400 years would have read.

The Lord is my shepherd: I shall not want. He maketh me to lie down in green pastures: he leadeth me beside still water. He restoreth my soul: he leadeth me in the paths of righteousness for his name's sake. Yea, though I walk through the valley of the shadow of death, I will fear no evil: for thou art with me. Thou preparest a table before me in the presence of mine enemies: thou anointest my head with oil;

The shepherd's calling was not just passed down to the male members of the family. Here a young shepherdess bottle-feeds an orphaned lamb.

my cup runneth over. Surely goodness and mercy shall follow me all the days of my life: and I will dwell in the house of the Lord for ever.

The shepherd will have understood this Psalm because it describes his working life, what he did for his sheep, and so through his own calling he could glimpse the very nature of God who cares for his people with the devotion of a shepherd.

The following account written in 1909 by Kate Henry-Anderson illustrates very eloquently the faith that shepherds had in God as the good and great shepherd of their souls:

On the hills above a small Highland town famous in history, there lived some years ago an old shepherd of the class now so rare. He was eighty-four years of age, hale and strong, with undimmed eyes and unclouded mind. In all his long life he had never been ten miles from the hamlet where he had a cottage, and he spent his days, and many nights, on the moors that stretch beyond Amulree.

Here in the long summer light you might find him with his two dogs, one a black-and-tan collie, the other a grey-and-white shaggy West Highland sheepdog; wise beasts that did all but speak. He carried in his 'pouch' or shepherd's bag, an old much-worn calf-bound Bible, and his peaceful leisure was well filled to him by the rhythm and grandeur of the Psalms of the Shepherd King who ages before watched his father's flocks.

The old man had been just such another youth 'ruddy and of fair countenance'; but glory, its perils and temptations, had passed him by, and left his soul free from the world's dark stain. The secret sweet influence of the Pleiads, the glory of the sun, moon and stars, the miracles of the seasons, and Nature's magical beauty, had wrought in him a simple faith, a serenity of mind and heart that were plainly written in his clear, gentle eyes and on his noble brow, that heritage of the true Scotch peasant. Fresh-coloured, tall and spare, with the muscular leanness that betokens a hardy outdoor life, only the snow-white hair and the many fine wrinkles of his face showed his great age.

He was a mine of tradition and folklore, and weather-wise to an extent that set his forecast far above the laird's barometer. I asked him once if he had never wished for a wider life, a sight of the unknown world that lay beyond the hamlet. 'Na, na,' he answered, with a genuine smile. 'I hae ma sheep an' the hills and the Psalms o' David dinna fail me. I want naething better. I'm never weary wi' them to read.' More than most men did he realise that the Lord was his shepherd. His soul has now gone to its eternal home and an old highland custom has set on the grey stone above the grave his humble calling after his name, thus:

ALASTAIR MACKENZIE
SHEPHERD
Who died aged 92
The Lord is my shepherd

★★★★★

One John Dundeney, a shepherd on the South Downs, even studied the Bible in Hebrew, having taught himself the language as he sat watching his flocks and once that was achieved, he taught himself astronomy. At a time when most peasants were illiterate, this shepherd, not from the school-room but from his own efforts on the hillside, had entered the world of the written word with the Bible as his text; he picked away at each and every word until he could read. This great achievement demonstrates graphically the patient nature of the shepherd. I once tried to teach myself the Welsh language and soon abandoned the undertaking, even though I had education and books to guide me.

Shepherds are known for their amazing powers of observation, which stems from their craft, as the shepherd has to be the keenest of observers, knowing each of his sheep individually, by sight, and by their particular behaviour, no matter the size of the flock. As a result he can spot early signs of ill health and act before the case is beyond remedy. This gift for observation is also applied to the world around the shepherd, who will know his country like the back of his hand, living his entire life on the same farm in the same parish and, until recently, rarely travelling more than ten miles from home.

As a result he would know every tree, every bush, every rabbit burrow, he would know when it was going to rain, where the snow would lie deepest and even, when a hedgerow had been grubbed out, he would tell you forty

Bedouin shepherds keeping their flocks in exactly the same manner as David, the writer of the Psalm 23.

years later where each tree and shrub had once stood – here a young oak, there an ash. This depth of local knowledge was often called upon to settle boundary disputes among neighbours, arguments over rights of way or quarrels over water rights, the word of the shepherd being respected and his honesty being beyond dispute.

The shepherd was a remarkably fit person and they needed to be. For example, in 1851, recorded in the publication *Pictorial Half Hour*, seventeen shepherds died in a single night during a savage winter storm.

It was the long walks over rugged terrain and the exposure to all weathers which made these men so hale and hearty, even into old age. James Gardner (1840–1900) was a shepherd and famous Collie dog trainer, mentioned in several accounts written down after his death. Here is his posthumous tribute.

An Appreciation by a Grateful Pupil, 1909

Mr. James Gardner belonged to one of the oldest shepherd families in Scotland. He was born in the Upper Ward of Lanarkshire, at a place called Todholes, in the year 1840, and died at North Cobbin-shaw, Midlothian, in 1900. He was deeply devoted to his calling, and would have regarded as an insult any suggestion or offer of social advancement which would have entailed his leaving the shepherd world. A true mountaineer, he retained a lofty independence, nor could he tolerate any of the forms of cant and hypocrisy. He was in the best sense a God-fearing man, but made no parade of religion. It was said of him at his death by one who knew him thoroughly:

'A truer and more generous man than James Gardner I have not known; he was quite incapable of mean action.' This very accurately summed up the character of the man. In company he was the very soul of good fellowship, his conversational powers being quite unique. Education and social opportunities would have made him a

great orator; the want of these gave him place and power in a humbler and purer world.

'Give me,' he would say with fine rustic eloquence, 'the warmth of my home and the devotion of my dogs and I will ask none of the vain and fleeting pleasures of the gay world.' When he died his dogs mourned his departure with all the pathos of loving and broken-hearted children.

James Gardner married when he was in his eighteenth year, his bride, Mary Black being in her seventeenth. They had four children, two sons and two daughters. His death was the result of an accident which happened when he was directing the demolition of an old building, and his wife survived him only a year. Much of an abstract nature has been written of the shepherd and his calling, but an experience of Mr. and Mrs. James Gardner's hospitality revealed in a memorable way all the sweetness and charm of life among the hills. Their guests were made to feel that warm hearts can convert small cots into great palaces.

Another appreciation of James Gardner by the Rev. Hugh Young, 1910:

It was in the spring of 1884 that I first became acquainted with Mr. James Gardner of North Cobbinshaw, and quickly formed a friendship close and intimate, which continued unbroken till his death. Daily intercourse with him soon made apparent his fine and sterling qualities as a man, and his unmatched skill and ability as a shepherd.

Among my first impressions of him, which remained and deepened as the years went on, were his genial nature, his kindly heart, his fidelity to duty, his intense interest in all things human, and his fine sympathy with every living thing in Nature, and, above all, in the flocks of sheep under his charge. He was possessed of a rich fund of folk-lore, as well as a varied, accurate, and extensive knowledge of all animals he came in contact with.

To me it was a sincere pleasure to hear him talk by his own fireside of the people of his acquaintance, and with the aid of a bright and vivid imagination describe in glowing language the humorous incidents of his shepherd life. Time and again was this done with unfailing interest, for the fund of stories was inexhaustible, and his powers of description brilliant.

I remember well and gratefully his kindly interest in myself when, coming to the district as a clergyman, a stranger, he took me in, not only to his home but to his heart, and not a little encouragement did I receive from him when I observed that he seemed to regard my work of a pastor as being carried very much on the lines of his own, although admittedly in different spheres, and I had always the feeling that his inward criticism of myself took the same direction; his ideal of a shepherd and his duties was high, and it was the strenuous effort of his life to attain it. His fidelity to and care over his flock were unapproachable and his knowledge of sheep and shepherd duties could not be surpassed.

Often when discoursing to my people on the Great and Good Shepherd have I had Mr. Gardner in my mind, and have drawn from the admirable, I might say perfect, manner in which he tended his flock my best points and aptest illustrations.

But even still more remarkable than his wonderful ability as a shepherd, was the extraordinary mastery he had over his dogs, as seen in his skill in training and managing them. It was extremely interesting to see him working them on the hill-side, or indeed anywhere. Every turn, every move seemed perfect; the reasons for this were probably the close intimacy and the friendly understanding that existed between the parties concerned, the master and his servants, and also the fact that he never struck his dogs; he had a dread of doing so, no matter how much they were at fault, or how they had disobeyed.

You may think Mr Gardner too much of a paragon of virtue to be true, judging by the generous opinions of others, but my research into shepherds has shown me that Mr Gardner was typical, rather than an exception, of this marvellous breed of men. If they have only one lesson for us today, it is the lesson of contentment, for these men had such small lives,

James Gardner (1840–1900). A good man and a fine Scottish shepherd.

the entirety of which was spent within a few square miles in a humble dwelling, with few possessions, yet they wanted nothing more.

Today people have such vast lives, full of travel and an array of possessions. Yet the shepherd in his humble, simple world with his faith, his sheep and his dogs, had a peaceful spirit and a vibrant soul that was refreshed daily by the poetry of nature. Today men seem to have such restless spirits and far less contentment. The old shepherds had so little, yet so very much; whereas today modern man has everything but seems to have so little. Does the shepherd not show us that the contentment we all seek is not in the vastness and abundance of life but in the little things that are so often overlooked?

CHAPTER THREE

The Nature of the Shepherd's Dog

THE SHEEPDOG, whatever its breed, is a mixture of intelligence, devotion, spirit, cunning, wit and courage, all combined for one purpose: to serve a master. The famed Ettrick Shepherd (James Hogg 1770–1835) wrote of sheepdogs:

'A single shepherd and his dog will accomplish more in gathering a stock of sheep from a Highland farm, than twenty shepherds could do without dogs; and it is fact, that, without this docile animal, the pastoral life would be a mere blank. Without the shepherd's dog, the whole of the open mountainous land in Scotland would not be worth a sixpence. It would require more hands to manage a stock of sheep, gather them from the hills, force them into houses and folds, and drive them to markets, than the profits of the whole stock would be capable of maintaining. Well may the shepherd feel an interest in his dog; he it is, indeed, that earns the family's bread, of which he is himself content with the smallest morsel; always grateful, and always ready to exert his utmost abilities in his master's interest.

Neither hunger, fatigue, nor the worst of treatment, will drive him from his side; he will follow him through fire and water, as the saying is, and through every hardship, without murmur or repining, till he literally fall down dead at his master's foot.'

Despite the invention of off-road vehicles it is still the case today that, without the sheepdog, the keeping of sheep in this undulating nation would be almost impossible. The following story is so remarkable it is hard to believe, but the event took place over 125 years ago, and was witnessed by numerous reliable people and recorded for posterity. This story was widely known in the area of Peebles for many decades and has been referred to as an example of the Collie's sagacity. But it goes far beyond the demonstration of the dog's perception and wisdom, for it also shows with great clarity the tremendous spirit with which the sheepdog is blessed.

There was a Mr Steel in Peebles, a Flesher, which is an old Scottish term for a butcher, and butchers relied on sheepdogs in much the same way as shepherds before the widespread use of lorries, to drive the flocks they purchased from the remote farms down the tracks, lanes and roads to the slaughter house. I do not know the name, nor do I have a description of the Collie bitch who is to be the star of our story but Mr Steel, upon purchasing sheep from a farmer, would put the entire, valuable flock in the charge of his single dog and command her to take them by herself, no matter what the distance, from the remote location of the farm to the flesh-market in Peebles.

While she was doing this, Mr Steel would then take a glass of something with the farmer to seal the deal, before setting off to settle further business affairs about the district, confident in the knowledge that his dog would deliver the sheep he had just bought safely to the slaughter-house, no matter what obstacles or distractions lay in her way. And this she did, year after year, till the day when Mr Steel placed a drove of sheep in his dog's charge at a farm called Willenslee, almost five miles from Peebles.

Mr Steel went about his business absolutely convinced that the sheep would be delivered to the Peeble's slaughter-house as usual. Upon returning home that evening Mr Steel was astonished to discover that his faithful dog had never turned up with the expected flock of sheep, which should have arrived many hours previously. Mr Steel, his son and a household servant, prompted by a great concern for the

This family photograph shows how shepherds considered their dogs to be fully-fledged members of the family. The family would no more have considered leaving the dogs out of this picture than they would the children, which is why the sheepdog is so fully committed to its family and why it takes prodigious care of the children.

missing dog, decided to set out to search for her, each man to take a different route for they didn't know which way the resourceful Collie would come. But just as they were about to set off, to their infinite relief the flock appeared in the distance, being driven at a steady walk down the empty street. The gate to the stockyard was opened and the Collie diligently yarded them but to everyone's astonishment she was carrying in her mouth a newborn pup.

Once sure that the sheep were safely penned, she retired to her kennel, placed the pup in the straw and took off back to the hills at high speed. Mr Steel, his son and servant were so taken aback that they made no attempt to stop her, despite the fact that she had obviously whelped earlier that day.

After some time the bitch returned another little pup softly carried in her mouth which was delivered to the kennel alongside the other pup, which was now being tended by Mr Steel's wife. The shepherd's wife had barely time to praise the bitch before she once more disappeared, only to return once more with another pup. This amazing bitch returned to the hill time and again, despite her exhaustion, until the entire litter was retrieved.

There is no agreed record as to the number of pups but Collie's have anything between six and twelve in a litter, so she more than likely had at least six trips back and forth to the hillside and maybe as many as twelve. The only sad note to this story is that the last pup to be brought home was dead, a fact which the bitch must have known yet still she felt it was her duty to bring it home.

This story illustrates marvellously so many of the qualities the sheepdog possesses, including truly remarkable physical endurance. The bitch in question had driven a flock of sheep five miles and somewhere along the route she had given birth to a litter with all the physical stress and pain which that involved. Then she had returned to the hill over and again to retrieve her entire litter, so she must have covered at least twenty additional miles of rugged terrain, a phenomenal physical achievement.

The sheepdog performs incredible deeds involving self-sacrifice, courage and a high level of intelligence because it loves its master, that love being written clearly in its countenance that brings delight to the heart of the shepherd whenever he looks upon his dog.

This story also shows the sheepdog's high level of intelligence: she had in her charge a large flock of sheep whose instinct, had the opportunity presented itself, was to return in an instant to the farm where they were born and reared. Had they for a moment felt that the dog could no longer hold them, they would have bolted back, so this bitch had to plan to hold the flock in some natural corral along the route which she had selected to enclose the sheep on three sides, with a narrow entrance across which the bitch could position herself to give birth and to repel any sheep that dared explore the entrance with a view to a possible escape. The level of forethought and planning involved in this undertaking is remarkable and far beyond the powers which most people ascribe to dogs but this sheepdog and others of her kind show that the sheepdog is indeed a thinking animal.

★★★★★

There is a rather macabre story which illustrates the thinking ability of the sheepdog, though in this case it is not a quality to be admired. There was a small, sly-looking Collie who did its work to great effect for her master, taking prodigious care of his sheep. But every now and again this Collie would just disappear and no one knew where she had gone till one day she was spotted returning home, pausing for a moment to wash herself in a stream. The witness to this noticed that the dog was soaked in blood.

At first the onlooker thought that the dog might be hurt and in need of assistance but it was quickly obvious that she was perfectly fine. It eventually emerged that sheep in the district were being savaged by a dog and this particular sheepdog was always missing around the time the attacks took place. Sheepdogs have a very well-established sense of right and wrong and this particular Collie must have known she was breaking the number one commandment for a sheepdog, which is to do no harm to sheep. Had she the foresight to cover her crime by trying to wash the blood off in a stream? Either way she paid the price for her misdemeanour with her life. No shepherd can keep a dog which kills sheep.

★★★★★

Even when too old to work on the hills by the side of the shepherd, the sheepdog in times past found a way to continue its devotion by becoming a yard dog, a dog which protects the shepherd's interests on his holding or his croft: this includes protecting the crops and keeping watch over the shepherd's children while they played outside.

To the shepherd pre-1940, his vegetable patch and few small fields of oats or barley were an essential part of his existence, providing much of the food needed for him and his family. Rabbits or birds could decimate the shepherd's fields and in a time before fencing was used to enclose crops, anything from a stray cow to an escaped pig could cause havoc in a field. So the sheepdog, too old and stiff to take to the hills, would guard the fields and the home with a steely determination, tackling any trespasser whether man or beast and guarding the crops.

My own two Collie dogs have a most peculiar habit of watching the skies around my smallholding, looking skywards on a regular basis, something I have never observed in any other dogs, not even the many gundogs I have known. My Collies are looking for birds, and if birds happen to land on my field, the Collies go charging off to scare them away. I believe this is an instinct from the work their ancestors used to do, crop guarding, and it is fascinating to watch.

Most people see the sheepdog purely as a dog for the handling of sheep but the retired sheepdog also once had a guarding role, protecting all that belonged to the shepherd from his potato fields to his prize ram. The old Collies' role in keeping a watchful eye on the shepherd's young children was invaluable to the shepherd's wife, who would often be responsible for milking a cow, tending chickens, attending to kitchen duties and the washing of clothing, to mention only a few of the duties she had to perform to keep the croft or farmhouse running smoothly. She could not be expected to always have a watchful eye on the children who could get into all kinds of mischief and farms can be very dangerous places for children. Modern health and safety records have revealed that for one recorded year (2003) 35 children died in farm-related fatal accidents, with many more being injured.

Another quality of the remarkable sheepdog is courage, shown over and again by their regular appearance in the Roll of the Dickin Medal, the animal-equivalent of the Victoria Cross. One such brave sheepdog was Nipper whose act of bravery was performed in 1985.

Before I relate Nipper's story, let me tell you about a fire that happened on a farm not more than two miles from mine, which suddenly engulfed a large stock-shed containing hundreds of sheep. As the fire took hold, the poor creatures' panic set in, neutralizing what little intelligence a sheep has. Instead of them trying to find a way out, they huddled in a corner, where of course they perished.

Yet I have seen sheep in pursuit of a particular piece of grazing, jump a 4ft fence; and there are numerous accounts of sheep, after having been sold, returning to the farm on which they were born, involving a journey of dozens of miles over all manner of obstacles and terrains: yet not a single sheep in this local fire jumped from its pen and escaped. They were killed as much by fear as they were by the fire.

Nipper's act of courage involves a fire. On a farm in Sussex, a huge barn caught alight, and the 370 stock inside,

The courage shown by Nipper and Fly is a quality found in all sheepdog breeds, which is why so many of them have found new employment as guard dogs, like this German shepherd which served in the Royal Air Force.

made up of ewes with lambs, and cows with calves, were destined to perish as the fire spread rapidly, fuelled by the straw and hay. Nipper, protecting his master's stock, rushed into the burning barn and despite the same fear that the fire had instilled in the sheep and cattle, Nipper mastered them and drove them through the flames to safety, guiding the beasts along a route which in their panic they would never have found.

Time and again Nipper had to return to the barn bringing out the stock in small manageable groups, burning his paws severely in the process on the red-hot straw over which he had to dash. Nipper saved all but nine of the 370 animals housed in the barn, testament not only to his great courage but to his determination and cool-headedness. Out of interest I have done a little bit of training with my two Collies around fire, to see how they behaved. They did not like the fire at all, giving it as wide a berth as possible and displaying a natural antipathy towards the flames which I have also observed in horses.

Nipper, the hero of our story, would have been no different: but that same antipathy he must have suppressed and tackled one of nature's most dangerous enemies. The only force which would overcome that inbuilt, natural and perfectly sensible fear, a fear which leads to self-preservation, is love and devotion, the most powerful forces in existence, which the sheepdog has in great abundance.

★★★★★

There was a sheepdog bitch by the name of Fly who, just three days after whelping, dashed to the aid of her master who was being attacked by a bull; this in Victorian times, when bulls still proudly sported their enormous and often deadly horns. Fly heard the cries of her master in distress and

The intuition, intelligence and devotion of sheepdogs explains why they were chosen to pioneer the use of guide dogs for the blind.

dashed across the farm like a speeding bullet, leaping at the bull, snarling, snapping then biting him in the fetlocks to make him turn away from the injured farmer. Had she not acted instinctively, Fly's master would have been gored to death. Not all acts carried out by sheepdogs involve infernos or aggressive bulls: but the sheepdog simply uses its natural instincts all the time, whatever the circumstances.

Such was the case of Hughie Roberts in 1934 who had recently moved to a new Welsh hill farm beyond Aberystwyth. He was attending a neighbour's funeral which took place some miles away from his farm. Mr Roberts had taken his sheepdog with him and stayed overnight after the funeral. The following day dawned to a heavy snowfall and Mr Roberts, despite being unfamiliar with the area, set out on his return journey.

Gradually he realized to his horror that the tracks in the snow were his own and that he was going round in circles. He was disorientated and lost on the hillside. His dog sensed his master's concern, picking up on the fear and confusion his master betrayed through his expressions, movements and tone of voice, all of which a good dog can read like an open book. Quietly, the dog took the lead with a simple glance at his master that seemed to say: *follow me*. Though this dog had travelled the route only once before, he knew his way home and acted as a guide all the way back, to the great relief of Mr Roberts who now owed his life to his dog.

To the sheepdog, this type of devotion is for life, a lesson that humans have not learnt, withdrawing love for the most trivial of reasons. The devotees of evolution believe that a dog is nothing more than a flesh and blood machine, programmed by survival instincts and DNA, to seek its own ends and comfort. The preceding stories indicate that the dog is so much more than that; that the sheepdog has its own soul, manifest every day of his life, through a love of its master and a devotion to duty.

CHAPTER FOUR

The Shepherd and his Sheep

Many people will tell you that sheep are stupid creatures, with not enough brains in an entire flock to fill a matchbox, but this is the view of those with scant knowledge of sheep. If they had spent much time watching them, as shepherds do, they might think otherwise.

Sheep can be trained to carry out all manner of tasks. We once had on our smallholding a young Suffolk ram, trained to walk to heel like a dog. Every day it accompanied us on our dog walks, playing with the dogs and coming when called. This very affectionate ram had been hand-reared by us, starting its early life living in our dining room where it was warm and where it could receive its four bottle-feeds a day. The ram went by the name of Punch, to which it always responded, and was a delightful and playful friend with a deeply inquisitive nature. His company was enjoyed by all the family till the sad day when he died unexpectedly, at less than a year old.

Sheep quite often suddenly die without reason, as many shepherds will tell you. It was something of a blessing in disguise because not long after the death of Punch, the devastating foot and mouth outbreak spread across the country and although our stock did not have foot and mouth disease, the regulations required that they be slaughtered.

Muffin was another great character we owned, a Lleyn Valley cross. At birth, he was tiny and close to death when he was given to us: his mother had died in labour. My mother, who is an expert at bottle-feeding orphaned lambs (known in Wales as 'Mollies') reared this pathetic little creature in the dining room at the same time as I was rearing a baby barn owl in the study, so the house was filled with the bleating of the lamb and the screech of the owl, both demanding food at regular intervals. Muffin was pure mischief, always finding something to upturn or search out, and he had a proud way of lying down on a bale of straw like a king seated upon his throne. I mention these lambs that I have known well, simply to illustrate the fact that a sheep is not just meat walking around on four legs but a vivid and lively character, something that the shepherds of old understood and often alluded to in their conversation and writings.

Some of these shepherds tended as many as three hundred sheep, yet they could still identify each and every one, not by some number tagged to an ear but by the character displayed and the markings and appearance of each sheep. On breeds like the Scottish Black Face, this is easier because the markings vary from sheep to sheep, helping with identification; but on a breed like the Wiltshire Horn, which has the same colouration over its entire body, identification is more difficult. Yet a shepherd could still carry in his head such information as which ewes had had triplets, which had broken its leg last winter and which part of the hill was a particular sheep's favourite grazing spot.

The shepherd's knowledge of his flock has even been accepted as expert evidence in court in cases of sheep stealing, which was once a hanging crime. This fact is testament to the shepherd's knowledge of his flock being considered infallible. The sheer volume of facts and information a shepherd used to hold within his head is staggering: they could if asked recall the entire genealogy of a flock going back ten, twenty or even thirty years, which would involve enormous numbers depending on the size of the flock.

Punch the young Suffolk ram who behaved just like one of the family' pet dogs.

It is recorded that the shepherd, unlike many others in pre-Victorian Britain, knew how to read and many used this ability to build on the skills and knowledge vested in him by previous generations, through studying books such as the *Complete Modern Farrier*, which had a detailed section on ailments affecting sheep, with chapters on the diseases of the head, chest, abdomen and external parts, and further chapters on gestation, birth and feeding, all areas in which the shepherd must be a complete expert.

Herd animals

Sheep are gregarious, herd animals, needing the company of their own kind to be happy, although sheep will happily mix with a herd of goats, and individual sheep are sometimes purchased to be a companion to horses, the two becoming inseparable friends. The leader of a flock of sheep is always an elderly matriarchal ewe who knows every single path and blade of grass upon her ground, capable of leading the flock along mountain tracks; sometimes with steep drops on either side. If you look at fields in which lowland sheep have walked, you will notice the paths that they use to get from

Muffin seated regally upon a bale of straw like a king upon his throne.

one part of the field to the other and in wet weather you will observe that the sheep follow almost exactly in the footsteps of one another. I have always wondered why lowland sheep follow one another in this manner, at times following the matriarch as closely as if their lives depended on it, when the fields they are in are so obviously safe, but I suppose it is the old instinct left behind from the time when all sheep lived on hills.

It is worth exploring why sheep move around in flocks. It is as a means of protection, the many eyes and ears being able to spot and evade predators more successfully than a single pair of eyes and ears. However, it is a residual precaution, for it has been many hundreds of years since sheep in Britain have needed to protect themselves from serious predators like the wolf and the lynx or even the bear which existed on these shores until the tenth century.

A thousand years after the loss of such predators, sheep still operate as a flock, so is there more to be gained from being in a flock than simple protection? From conversations I have had with numerous shepherds, I believe that this is in fact the case.

Consider a sheep that for some reason or other goes blind, becoming especially helpless if it is a mountain sheep where it could easily wander over a sheer drop. The blind animal is always adopted by another member of the flock who, between grazing, can be seen to keep a constant eye on the blind creature, bleating a warning whenever it goes too close to the edge. When the flock moves off, the blind sheep is not left behind but is called by the one who has adopted it. The blind sheep is able to home in on the bleating of its friend.

If for some reason the blind sheep fails to follow when called, its 'guardian' leaves the flock and, like a guide dog, gathers up the blind sheep and leads it back to the flock.

Unbelievable as it may sound, it is true and I have even observed this behaviour in young lambs under eight weeks old. To recognize the fact that one of their fellow creatures is blind shows a high level of observation but to realize that it therefore needs assistance shows a high degree of intelligence.

Survival of the flock

Sheep also show even greater compassion for one another by the demonstration of a self-sacrificing nature for the preservation of the flock. There was a disease before the advent of inoculations known by old shepherds as 'breakshugh', a form of dysentery which can spread through a flock of sheep like an inferno through a barn of hay. Many of the shepherds who had first-hand experience of this disease in their flocks reported that when a sheep felt its onset, the doomed creature would take itself far away from the flock, shunning contact with other sheep to prevent the infection spreading.

The shepherds have also commented that these diseased sheep hide themselves away so well that they are very hard to find, even with the aid of sheepdogs. For a creature so dependent on the company of its own kind to withdraw at a time of illness, when its natural desire must be to stay close to the flock from which it derives comfort, shows that the sheep puts the preservation of the flock far above its own needs.

The shepherd's vocation

Watching animals going about their daily activities is somehow therapeutic to man's spirit, whether watching horses frolicking in a field or ducks bathing in a pond; but there is something especially rewarding about watching new born lambs discover the spring in their young legs as they leap with joy across a hillside.

The blind lamb above was adopted and watched over by the lamb beside it. Even the goats in the next pen took an interest in the welfare of the blind lamb.

A shepherd's job tended to be a lifetime's vocation, a life he enjoyed, having no desire to change his occupation. Ralph Fleesh wrote in 1909 about Irish shepherds, *'Proud of his calling, the supreme desire of the Irish shepherd is to live till the end comes with his dogs and sheep.'* Sheep, dogs and nature brought a trinity of contentment to the shepherd.

Rescue from a mountain-ledge

A good shepherd needs to understand the psychology of the sheep. For example, sheep always have an eye for the juiciest blade of grass they can find and sometimes that happens to be growing on the side of a mountain on a ledge barely wide enough for the sheep to stand, on the edge of an almost sheer drop. Somehow the eagle-eyed sheep, having spotted the tempting blade of grass, makes its way down to the ledge and once the morsel is consumed, the creature then discovers that coming down there might have been difficult but getting back up is impossible, no matter how hard it tries.

The shepherd doing his rounds spots the sheep trapped on the mountain ledge, and he carefully observes its position but does nothing to rescue it. Days go by, the sheep is hungry but the shepherd still does nothing but watch.

To an onlooker this might seem heartless but the shepherd knows his sheep and is fully aware that if he were to throw down a rope and lower himself onto the ledge to rescue the sheep at this stage, when it is still fit, it would take fright, seek to escape and plunge to its death. So the shepherd waits and watches till the day he hears the sheep crying for help with a constant bleating, then he waits still further until the sheep lies down exhausted by hunger and dehydration, in a state of pure submission, ready at last to be helped. Only then, and with the skill of an experienced rock climber, the shepherd will pick his way down the sheer face from one foothold to the next, working hand over hand down a rope till he stands besides the sheep on the ledge.

Usually a second rope would then be made into a secure harness and fastened firmly about the sheep's body, the weak creature now unable to kick or struggle, which could prove fatal for a shepherd if he were kicked off the narrow ledge. The shepherd would then climb back up, hauling his charge by hand, up the side of the mountain. A ewe weighing roughly thirty kilograms is an extremely physical challenge to pull up fifty feet: it requires great strength.

It is essential that the ewe is inert while she is hauled up the mountain-side. Mountains are unpredictable and diffi-cult to gauge in terms of danger: even on the most simple of climbs, men have fallen only thirty feet in the mountains and been killed; whilst others have fallen a thousand feet or more and suffered only a broken bone or two.

A good shepherd must have a head for heights and the courage to tackle challenging rock faces, which is why so many shepherds were involved in the early days of mountain rescue, when mountain rescue teams were first established.

Any shepherd going to the aid of a beleaguered sheep is risking his life to save it. Why does he bother? He has many more sheep and the financial loss of a single sheep which had placed itself in jeopardy would hardly ruin the shepherd. The sheep may be old, toothless, skinny, with a poor fleece and of little value, but she is one of the shepherd's flock, one of his responsibilities and he is duty-bound by the nature of his calling to protect them all.

Many shepherds have died carrying out their duty to their sheep, mostly in the wintertime, but from accounts handed down the threat of death never seems to deter them. The Ettrick Shepherd, James Hogg, was as fond of his sheep as any shepherd and he wrote many stories about country life in the nineteenth century. This story of his, witnessed by

The shepherd willingly risks his life on treacherous slopes to rescue his sheep.

many, demonstrates another quirk of the sheep which caused challenges for the shepherd: its desire to return to the hill on which it was born and raised.

'So strong is the attachment of sheep to the place where they have been bred, that I have heard of their returning from Yorkshire to the Highlands,' he wrote. [It must be remembered that this was written at a time when fencing was not used and there were no motorcars or motorways!] *'The most singular instance that I know of, to be authenticated, is that of a black ewe that returned with her lamb from a farm in the head of Glen-Lyon to the farm of Harehope in Tweeddale and accomplished the journey in nine days. She was soon missed by her owner, and a shepherd was despatched in pursuit of her, who followed her all the way to Crieff where he turned and gave her up.*

He got intelligence of her all the way, and every one told him that she absolutely persisted in travelling on. She would not be turned, regarding neither sheep nor shepherd by the way. Her lamb was often far behind, and she had constantly to urge it on, by impatient bleating. She unluckily came to Stirling on the morning of a great annual fair, about the end of May, and judging it imprudent to venture through the crowd with her lamb, she halted on the north side of the town the whole day, where she was seen by hundreds, lying close by the road-side.

But next morning, when all became quiet, a little after the break of day, she was observed stealing quietly through the town, in apparent terror of the dogs that where prowling about the streets. The last time she was seen on the road, was at a toll-bar near St Ninians; the man stopped her, thinking she was a strayed animal, and that some one would claim her. She tried several times to break through by force when he opened the gate, but he always prevented her, and at length she turned patiently back. She had found some means of eluding him, however, for home she came on a Sabbath morning the 4ᵗʰ of June; and she left the farm of Lochs, in Glen-Lyon, either on the Thursday afternoon, or Friday morning, a week and two days before. The farmer of Harehope paid the Highland farmer the price of her, and she remained on her native farm till she died of old age, in her seventeenth year.

This sheep had travelled roughly 150 miles.

★★★★★

Sheep are kept for their wool as well as their meat, the wool once being the most valuable part of the sheep. It was the early wool industry that made Britain so wealthy, the 1600 and 1700s being a particularly prosperous time.

One example of the commerce going on in wool during the 1790s clearly illustrates the worldwide demand for wool produced on these shores: the vast amounts of wool from mid-Wales that was sold to Russia in order to clothe its enormous army. The best way to understand the value of wool from Medieval times and for several centuries thereafter is to think of it in terms of oil today: what oil revenue has done for Arab countries, wool did for this country centuries ago.

Washing and shearing sheep

In order to get the wool from the sheep, the process of shearing had to be carried out, usually around July for hill sheep. But before the shearing could commence, the washing of the sheep had to take place, usually nine days or so before shearing.

The purpose of the washing was to remove the grease from the wool, as the cleaner the wool, the higher the price it acquired. The washing was brought about by driving the flock of sheep through a dammed-up stream or a naturally deep pool in a river. A corral was constructed on the river-bank to funnel the sheep toward the water and with men and dogs pushing hard from the rear, the sheep would take to the water. They have the ability to swim though they will stubbornly plant themselves on the riverbank to the very last minute. Shepherds were not keen on the sheep-washing as it involved a huge amount of work in the form of going to the mountain, time and again, to bring down each heft (group of sheep) in its turn for the washing.

The other reason that the shepherds did not favour this time of year was the numerous broken legs that occurred among the young lambs, during the pushing and shoving that went on as the flock was harried into the water.

The shepherd mended these broken legs by taking a branch from a birch tree and peeling the bark from the branch in one long strip, which was wrapped firmly around the lamb's leg and secured in place with strips of material to form a cast, made simply from nature's store cupboard.

This ability to take from nature that which is needed to cure his flock shows us that the shepherd of old was a very skilled herbalist. The bark from the birch tree is antiseptic so the casts they made would not only hold the leg firmly in place to allow the break to fuse, they would also prevent infection and putrefication and inhibit the growth of micro -organisms. It cannot be by chance that the shepherds took the bark from the birch: they could just as easily have taken the bark from another tree which did not posses such healing properties. These skills have been lost today, as the modern shepherd turns to manufactured drugs to heal his flock rather than turning to nature's medicine chest. It is quite interesting to note that it was not only the old shepherds who made use of the birch in this way: it was also a favourite tree of the American Indian who used its sap to make a much-valued horse tonic.

The hard work involved in getting the flock washed was often leavened by a bit of good humour, especially when a ewe running between a shepherd's legs managed to unbalance him, pitching him into the pool alongside his sheep. It was also not uncommon for a powerful ram to get one of its horns entangled in a shepherd's clothing and when it leapt into the water with purpose, the shepherd was propelled in with him.

The washing of sheep in this manner came to an end in the 1960s when mechanisation in the processing of the wool took over the job of cleaning the wool. Shearing was the time of year when the farm saw a mass influx of people all coming to help with the task, including neighbours, relatives from afar combining their yearly visit with the shearing, and tramps who roamed from farm to farm, following the shearing in search of ad hoc work.

At one farm in Wales called Nant-stalwen there were 200 people involved in the shearing of the farm's 6,000-strong flock and from this number of men, about 160 would have been carrying out the shearing whilst the other 40 would have been tending the waiting sheep. Each shearer would have to shear about 37 sheep each day, all of the work being done with hand shears.

Those doing the tending would mostly be boys, providing the shearers with string so that they could tie the legs of the sheep prior to commencing with the shearing.

The purpose of tethering the legs was to keep the sheep still for the shearing process – a dangerous time due to the sharpness of the implements.

As the shearing began, one man would be placed in charge of a fire over which pitch (a form of tar) was melted in order to brand the sheep with the farmer's mark, after they had been sheared. The pitch had to be just the right temperature – too hot and it would burn the sheep and too cool and would not make a discernible mark.

The pitch mark would last till autumn when the flock would once more be gathered and each one provided with a coloured raddle mark: this involved placing a dab or stroke of marking fluid in different places on the sheep, each farmer having his own unique pattern of marking. In years gone by the marking fluid would be made from natural substances, for example in the North Ceredigion area of Wales there was a rock that when crushed to a powder and mixed with animal fat formed a bluish paste.

Shearing by hand is a very skilled and physical process that began with the shearing of the under-belly, then the neck, moving on to the left side shearing from belly to backbone. The shepherd then returned to the neck and clipped down it onto the right side of the sheep which was again clipped from belly to backbone.

Once shorn, the sheep was carried away and laid on a bed of rushes, which fulfilled two objectives: firstly the sheep after losing its deep protective outer coat would not be bruised and secondly it kept the freshly-shorn sheep nice and clean while it was marked with pitch. Then a responsible lad would untie the sheep and when he came to every tenth sheep he would shout out to the tally man 'Ten sheep': in Wales he would of shouted 'Deg dafad'.

The tally man was a highly-respected member of the community who had the vital job of making an inventory of the flock. This he did in the time-honoured way on a length of stick about 20in in length and ½in square on which he would make a cross marking for every ten sheep on one side of the stick and on the other sides of the stick he would make markings for each wether (castrated ram) and each ram. The completed stick would thus hold an inventory of the entire flock, the information being kept in strictest confidence by the tally man who would not divulge the information to any

Sheep-washing in a stream to clean the wool prior to shearing.

other but the owner of the flock and his shepherds.

Accidentally cutting a sheep whilst shearing was frowned on and if it occurred more than once, the shearer was often relieved of his duties and asked to do a spell in the catching pens.

Women and the shearing

Not only did the men work extremely hard during the shearing but the women as well, who would have to make sufficient food for the small army of workers. This traditionally involved the provision of one loaf of bread per man, meat in the form of a calf or numerous wethers slaughtered for the purpose with some of the meat being roasted and some boiled. Rice pudding was always a feature of shearing days and would be made by the bucketful and no shearing day would have been properly catered for without the provision of cake of the rich fruit variety, the following being the traditional shearing recipe as used by Mrs Cecilia Jones of Llanarth.

The Shearer's Loaf

12 quarts of flour
5 pounds of butter
2 pounds of lard
5 pounds of currents
4½ pounds of sultanas
7½ pounds of demerara sugar
2 oz of nutmeg and spice
½ pound of lemon peel
14 eggs
½ ounce of yeast
a glassful of rum
milk

This huge mixture must have been made in a very large vessel of some kind by a strong women as the mixture made about 12 very large cakes, sufficient to meet the needs of about 100 people.

When the shearing was finished and everyone had been well-fed, the evening would give way to singing and reciting as the labourers recharged their batteries for the following day of shearing on another farm usually about a mile or so away.

The shearing in each small district would last about a fortnight, each farm having its turn according to an order that had been established back in the mists of time, now set

The shearing completed and all the fleeces loaded up for delivery.

in stone. The shearing was the major part of the shepherd's financial year as he harvested wool like other farmers harvested wheat.

Shearing time served to bring communities together in a common purpose, everyone working to bring about the prosperity of an area of countryside. This joint purpose built a community spirit that gave an even greater richness to these remote and beautiful rural areas where people had to depend upon one another completely. This way of life and the community that it fostered are now dead and gone forever, because today a gang of ten shearers with electrical shears can go though thousands of sheep quicker than the hundreds of local people who laboured by hand. Modern shearing gangs sometimes even come from the Antipodes, so shearing has become a commercial venture, the social aspect having completely vanished.

Progress may have brought us many valuable benefits such as better living conditions, healthcare and more prosperity but it has come at a cost in rural areas, in terms of loss of community spirit and inter-dependence.

The old rural shepherding community lived isolated lives for much of the year, but at such times as shearing, the people came together to refresh and enrich one another

CHAPTER FIVE

The Shepherd and Sheepdog at War

In 1914 the country was rocked by the outbreak of a war across Europe that everyone, from the mountains of Scotland to the corridors of London's parliament, thought would be over by Christmas. How wrong they were! Later given the title of the Great War, the only great thing about it was the courage of the men and dogs who fought so bravely.

At the beginning the war, shepherds were not conscripted and the army had no use for their dogs. One man, even before the war had started, had been trying his best to persuade those in the War Office that soldiers needed the help of highly-trained dogs in order to maintain fluid lines of communication.

This lone voice belonged to dog trainer Edwin Hautonville Richardson but the War Office ignored his suggestions, believing that there could be no place in modern warfare for a dog, surely not to be relied upon to carry vital messages between the troops and headquarters; nor could a dog be expected to perform diligently under the heavy bombardment which was to be such a major feature of this war; those in high office believing that the dogs would turn tail and run, under an onslaught of shells.

The army preferred to put their confidence in human runners and in telephone communications, which relied entirely on wires to connect the phones. But it soon emerged at the Front that the very first shells of a bombardment disabled the phone wires, blowing them to pieces and breaking the flow of communication, so human runners had to take messages from the forward positions back to headquarters instead. This meant a man running through a hail of shell-fire and bullets, over shell-pitted ground, scrambling over barbed wire and across water-filled ditches, sometimes at night.

The job of the runner turned out to be one of the most dangerous jobs of the war. The exposure to fire of these young men, singled out for their athleticism, was so great that they often lasted only a couple of days. And of course when the runners died on their mission, the message they were carrying failed to get through.

But despite Richardson's constant representations to members of the High Command, they refused to listen to his argument that trained, working dogs could take the place of these runners, doing the job in a fraction of the time and with far fewer casualties.

The German army meanwhile had no such reservations about using dogs: in fact prior to the war, German secret agents were sent to England and they travelled about the country buying up the finest sheepdog puppies they could find, sending them back to Germany to become recruits for the army under the training of the Der Verein Für Deutsche Schäferhunde, the German national dog training association, which was run by high-ranking German military officers.

Richardson did what little he could, working with the French army, which had small dog units used for the carrying of messages, and this proved very successful. Richardson learnt a lot from this experience, observing the dogs from these units in action under heavy fire, and he was very impressed by their courage and singleness of purpose.

As the war ground on, by 1917 the British Army was suffering a severe shortage of men and equipment. In desperation, the War Office finally opened up talks with Richardson to see if he could train dogs to carry messages, for no other reason than that it would save the lives of the runners. Richardson responded with alacrity and set up a dog training centre at Shoeburyness, close to where the artillery trained, so that the dog recruits would be constantly within earshot of the guns used for training.

The first thing that Richardson requested was men to work as dog training instructors, who would be able to train dogs and their handlers at the same time. For instructors, Richardson wanted men from one of three civilian professions: staff from hunts kennels who were used to training large numbers of dogs; gamekeepers who were experienced in training dogs to work around gunfire; and shepherds who knew how to make dogs work independently, at a distance from their handler.

Richardson later wrote that the kind of dog training carried out in peacetime which came closest to the training of army messenger dogs was the training of the shepherd's dog.

Messenger dog Nell waits patiently for the officer on the left to write a message before making a day-time run back to H.Q. Nell was a sheepdog who carried many messages through the worst of the fighting and is officially credited with saving thousands of lives.

And so, in response to Richardson's request, shepherds of experience gave up the quiet hills to help in the training of army dogs. For men who had barely travelled more than ten miles from their farms, moving to the barracks at Shoeburyness must have been something of a culture shock in itself.

It is interesting to note from the writings of Richardson that his dog-training philosophy was so much in line with the approach taken by shepherds in training their dogs. Regarding the training of army messenger dogs, he wrote:

The messenger dog has to be trained in such a way that it takes keenest delight and pride in its work. The highest qualities of mind – love and duty – have to be appealed to and cultivated. Coercion is of no avail for of what use would this be when the dog is two or three miles away from the keeper? [the average distance over which a dog had to carry a message.] *In fact it may be said that the whole training is based on appeal. To this end the dog is gently taught to associate everything pleasant with its working hours. Under no circumstances whatever must it be roughly handled or roughly spoken to. If it makes a mistake or is slack in its work when being trained, it is never chastised but is merely shown how to do it over again. If any of the men under instruction are observed to display roughness or lack of sympathy with the dogs, they should be instantly dismissed, as a promising young dog could easily be thrown back in his training or even spoiled altogether by sharp handling.*

It is remarkable that love was at the centre of a training programme for dogs which would be going to the blood, slaughter and hell of trench warfare. Nevertheless these dogs were trained with love, and they worked out of love for their masters throughout the darkness of war. It was Richardson and his instructors, many of whom were shepherds, who were the dog-trainers. So Richardson had his instructors: now he needed dogs, and by the hundreds. At first Battersea and Manchester dogs homes were the suppliers but very soon they could not meet the demand and so every suitable stray that was taken in by the police throughout the country was sent to be a war dog but still more were needed and so a nationwide appeal was launched to which the country magnificently responded, volunteering dogs of all kinds among which were some working sheepdogs.

Not all breeds, for obvious reasons, were acceptable, and Richardson's favourites were the Airedales, sheepdogs and lurchers. The following official list of a despatch of dogs sent to France gives a clear demonstration of the breeds that were deemed suitable for the work of a messenger dog.

Breed of Dogs	Number
Collies	74
Lurchers	70
Airedale	66
Sheepdogs	36
Retrievers	33
Irish terriers	18
Spaniels	11
Deerhounds	6
Setters	4
Welsh terriers	5
Bull Terriers	5
Greyhounds	2
Eskimos	2
Dalmatians	2
Bedlingtons	2
Pointers	2
Bulldogs	1
Whippets	1
Total	340

Dogs being taken down service trenches to the forward position. Even in this poor quality photo you can clearly see that the dogs are totally relaxed and at ease in this alien environment. The dogs committing the route to memory for the return journey which, would be under fire.

The listing of sheepdogs refers to working dogs of a non-Collie type which came from farms; and the listing of Collies refers to working dogs of the Border Collie type and non-working Collies of the pedigree type like the rough-coated Collie. The rather unusual listing of 'Eskimos' refers to the husky.

This list clearly shows that sheepdogs, whether from working or pedigree stock, were by far the most heavily-represented of the breeds, accounting for a third of this draft of army messenger dogs. Clearly both the shepherd and the working sheepdog played their role in the great conflict that was World War I.

Here is Richardson's official description regarding the role of the army messenger dog:

The modern bombardments, which are a feature of modern warfare, render communication with the front line exceedingly difficult to maintain. The object of the use of messenger dogs therefore is;

1. To save human life.

2. To accelerate dispatch-carrying.

Telephones soon become useless and the danger to the human runner is enormous. Added to the difficulties are the shell holes, the mud, the smoke and gas and darkness. It is here that the messenger dog is of the greatest assistance. The broken surface of the ground is of small moment to it as it lightly leaps from point to point. It comes to its duty in the field well broken to shell-fire and so has no fear. Its sense of direction is as certain at night as in the day and equally so in mist or fog. Being a smaller and more rapidly-moving object, the danger of its being hit is much less than in the case of a runner and it is a fact that during the war, casualties were extraordinarily low among the messenger dogs especially when it is taken into consideration that their work was always in the hottest of the fight. There is a most remarkable record of the tenacity and courage with which the dogs did their work in the face of every kind of difficulty. There have been many occasions when a situation at one moment so full of anxiety and uncertainty has been completely transformed by these brave dogs bearing their message of information and appeal.

At the war dog-training school, keepers were assigned three dogs each, for which they were fully responsible. This included exercise, feeding and grooming, in order to build up a strong bond between dogs and master, a bond structured around love and trust.

The keeper, under the careful tuition of the school instructors, would then begin to train the dogs in basic obedience and would daily take the dogs over to the artillery batteries where the dogs would not only get used to the sound but also the impact of the guns as they thundered out, rocking the ground like an earthquake.

This part of the training was done systematically and very carefully, so that the dogs got completely accustomed to the noise of the guns in a fairly short time. For the sheepdogs that had come from the remote hills, where the screech of an

Above: The shaggy looking dog on the left is messenger dog Tweed who was a working sheepdog and though he looks to modern eyes like a mongrel he is a recognized breed known as a Highland Sheepdog.

eagle as it glided above the valleys in search of prey would have been a more familiar sound, the noise of gunfire must have been a real shock to the system and it must have taken real skill and gentleness on the part of the instructor to get a timid-natured sheepdog to accept the noise of dozens of heavy artillery guns, hammering out shell after shell.

Once the dogs had become attached to their new keeper, they would be taken a short distance from him by the instructors and released, the keeper calling his dogs to him. Using this simple exercise, the distance would be increased steadily until the dogs were travelling three or four miles back to their keeper. The ground over which the dogs were trained was varied as much as possible and they were taught to travel along roads, amongst lorries and other traffic, through villages and past every sort of camp and cook-house temptation. They were taught not to be afraid of water or of any terrain.

To prepare the dogs for the Front, all manner of obstacles were introduced to the training runs such as barbed wire entanglements, palings, fences, water dykes and smoke-screens. Each dog was allowed to find its own way through and around the obstacles: there was no right or wrong way to proceed. All that mattered was that the dog returned to its keeper as quickly as it could, without stopping along the way.

The trainee dogs were exposed daily to rifle fire, having to run through a small squad of soldiers firing blanks. The dogs also had to carry out training runs under heavy artillery bombardment, thus fully preparing them for all the conditions under which they would be operating in France.

At the Front

Once sent to a sector in France, the keeper would remain at headquarters and a suitably trained soldier from the front line would take the dogs to the forward trenches, the dogs committing the route to memory through sight and smell, knowing where their master was waiting anxiously for their safe return.

When the Commanding Officer wished to pass on some intelligence across the trenches, a message would be placed in a metal canister attached to the dog's collar and the dog would be released. As trained, it would dash across the pitted ground with shells thundering down and shrapnel falling like snow in a blizzard, ignoring the smell of death and the sense of panic in the air.

Witness accounts of these dogs at work report the dogs were actually enjoying carrying out their duty! With wagging tail, the dog was soon back with its relieved keeper, who lavished praise on his canine partner as he retrieved the message, which was then hastily delivered to the intended recipient.

Many of the messages were of a routine nature such as: 'Send forward dry socks for the men' and yet others were absolutely vital and their prompt delivery at headquarters could mean the holding of the line and the saving of countless lives.

It is reckoned that the work of the messenger dogs enabled Commanders to consolidate advances and to repel attacks on the trench. The more important messages carried by the dogs brought vital re-enforcements, ammunition or ordered bombardments. If the Commanders had sent human runners, many lives would have been lost and many messages would have been undelivered. Many sheepdogs, acting as these messenger dogs, helped enormously in the war effort and saved many, many lives in the process.

After the war, the dog school was scaled down. The advent of radio communications made the messenger dog redundant but the role of the army dog changed and the German Sheepdog became the breed that was recruited.

Tweed the War Hero

The following is the verbatim account of a keeper named Private Reid, who explains the work done by a working sheepdog called Tweed:

'Today I had Tweed and Jock acting as Battalion Runners for Battalion Headquarters to Transport Lines and they have done splendid. I had Tweed up the line and he brought back a very important message through heavy shellfire. I am highly satisfied with my dog.

On May 2nd 1918 I was sent to the 18th Div. There were no dogs that had been up before. On May 2nd at 10pm the Hun came over on the Q.V.R – my dog was up at their Batt Hdqtrs. They were cut off from the London Regt; they released Tweed with the message 'Send up reinforcements and small round ammunition.' He came through a Bosch barrage – three kilometres in 10 mins. The French were sent up and filled the gaps and straightened out the line, otherwise Amiens would be in the hands of the Germans.

On May 8th I was with the Australians 48th Batt. They had moved forward, no runner could cross the open ground in the daytime – pigeons could not fly at night, so they sent for Tweed. He made three runs at night and on one of the runs he was out on patrol; they sent him back with a message 'The Germans are preparing for a raid' and spoiled the Hun's plans.'

The dog Tweed mentioned here performed some wonderful services. He was a Highland sheepdog and took rather longer to train than usual, owing to his highly sensitive nature; in fact he was nearly rejected altogether and it was only through the urgent representations of Richardson's wife, who assisted in the training of the dogs and who discerned Tweed's fine character, that he had been retained and his training completed. Patience and great gentleness in handling had eventually overcome Tweed's timidity and the sound management of Tweed by his keeper in the field brought this dog up to a very high standard.

Though the messenger dogs suffered surprisingly few fatalities in comparison to their human counterparts, the dangers were enormous and many dogs were killed, injured or gassed. But the gas for some reason did not have such a pronounced effect upon the dogs as it did on the men and any blindness the dogs suffered as a result tended to be temporary. Even more remarkably, when blinded by gas many dogs still managed to deliver their vital message despite considerable pain, coughing, with tears streaming from their eyes and in great distress but using some sixth sense to find their way back.

One messenger dog was even shot in the jaw, yet with it literally hanging off he completed his run, delivering his urgent message. His distraught keeper rushed the dog to the veterinary station where the vets immediately shot it to put it out of its misery, there being no chance of repairing the horrendous damage.

Another injured messenger dog returned loyally with its message but died of its wounds in its keeper's arms shortly afterward. The post-mortem revealed it had shrapnel lodged in its spine and a bullet in its neck, yet despite these terrible injuries it did not give way to death till its mission had been completed.

It is inspirational to see these wonderful qualities shining through in that dark place of death and destruction.

CHAPTER SIX

Famous Sheepdogs

A sheepdog can earn fame in one of two ways: firstly it can perform an act of such courage that it captures the imagination of the entire nation; or it can become a champion sheepdog, winning an international sheepdog trial, in which case its fame, though not universal, will be firmly established among the shepherding community for many generations to come.

Let's begin with the story of a sheepdog by the name of Sheila, who by an act of courage found herself at the centre of the nation's affections for a couple of weeks during the war with Hitler. It was a dark afternoon on 16th December 1944. At the base of the Cheviot hills, a blizzard was raging, obscuring the peaks. John Dagg was in his warm little cottage at the base of the hills, sitting comfortably in front of a roaring fire, talking with his wife who was preparing their meal. Sheila was lying in her kennel in a bed of straw when suddenly her ears pricked up, discerning the distant roar of aircraft engines. Mr Dagg now heard the same almighty noise and rushed to his door to see what was coming - the largest American bomber of World War II, flying barely higher than the roof-height as it burst through the cloak of snow. Mr Dagg's heart froze with the realization that the aircraft on its present course would never clear the Cheviots but would smash right into them.

As the plane passed directly above the house, the ground shook – then the aircraft disappeared into the blizzard. Moments later a mighty crash was heard. Mr Dagg waited for the subsequent explosion but it did not come. Mr

John Dagg and Shelia.

Dagg told his wife to go to the village to call an ambulance and get help, adding that he would go up the hill to see if anyone was still alive.

Mrs Dagg knew that climbing the hill in this blizzard was fraught with danger but that if any man had the skill and endurance for it, it was John Dagg. As she hurried down the lane to get help, John fastened his boots and wrapped up warmly, then went to fetch his dog, Sheila, who was waiting at her kennel door in anticipation.

"I'm going to need you up there to find them," he said, letting her loose.

John Dagg took on the north side of the Cheviot, a three mile face that presented a daunting challenge even on a summer's day with its steep precipitous crags and plunging drops, dominated by Bizzle Crag with its burn far below. To tackle such a crag in a blizzard that was restricting vision to no more than a few inches, was only possible for someone like John Dagg, who could have made his way up the deadly face blindfold, every facet and feature of the climb being etched into his memory. Even so great care had to be exercised for this was a free climb and one slip on the snow-covered rocks and John Dagg would plunge to his death. Even if he survived a fall, no-one would be able to find him in this storm till it was too late. John Dagg never once checked on the position of Sheila; she was like a mountain goat and would be close at hand even if he could not see her.

It took John Dagg one and a half hours to reach the summit, where the howling blizzard was even more savage and the cold so penetrating that it bit through his clothes to his very core, numbing his mind as well as his fingers and toes. John Dagg looked around: he could smell burning but he could not see the huge Flying Fortress. When she came into view, Sheila seemed very anxious, which suggested they were not far from their goal.

After about an hour of searching, John Dagg noticed a sudden excitement in his dog that told him there was someone close by, so he shouted out, and through the storm, a powerful figure appeared. Frank Moscrop, a local young shepherd, had come up from Southern Knowe, the farm where John's wife had gone to raise the alarm. After ensuring that an ambulance was summoned, Frank had taken his shepherd's crook and climbed the hill to go and help John Dagg in his search.

The two shepherds briefly discussed tactics, then began another search of the summit. As they scoured the hilltop, the smell of burning became more intense and the snow was blackened with soot. Both knew that the downed aircraft was extremely close, but they just could not locate it.

As if sensing the problem, Sheila suddenly left John's side and disappeared into the blizzard. Moments later the dog reappeared and, urging her master to follow, Sheila carefully led them to the huge, twisted and burning aircraft. Again, Sheila asked John to follow and led him away from the plane to a peat hag where four very cold and badly injured aircrew lay shocked and bewildered. Sheila had succeeded where the most earnest efforts of the shepherds had failed. She had found the airmen.

"Stay away from the plane," shouted the airmen to the two shepherds, "It is full of bombs and when they go up they will take the top off this mountain."

Frank, when he learned that there were another five aircrew missing, ignored the warning and forced his way into the smouldering aircraft to search for any other survivors but there were none to be found. John meanwhile tended to the men's wounds: a deep laceration to the scalp, badly damaged and bleeding feet, an injured back and a broken jaw. Making use of what was to hand, he turned parachute silk into very serviceable bandages by cutting it into long strips.

When all the airmen had been patched up to the best of John's ability, they began on foot the descent of the treacherous hill, with the blizzard now getting worse. John reached into his deep coat pocket and pulled out his field compass but the blizzard was too dense for him to see it, so John and Frank had to rely entirely on their instincts to send them in the right direction, knowing that a wrong turn could send the entire party plunging to their deaths. With John at the front, Frank at the rear and Shelia to one side, they slowly made their way through the ever-worsening snow. The party had to stop frequently for the exhausted and injured airmen to rest and, each time they did so, Sheila pushed among the airmen and they snuggled together for warmth. At length, after three hours of danger and icy temperatures, the party reached John Dagg's cottage, where Mrs Dagg was waiting to tend to the airmen. The man with an injured back was put straight to bed but the other three sat around the large kitchen table and, after a warming meal of bacon and eggs with plenty of hot sweet tea, soon felt warmed through and in a fit state to tell the story of their doomed flight.

They had set out on a bombing raid from an airfield in the south of England for Germany but, shortly after take-off, the weather became very bad and the entire squadron was ordered back to base. On the return journey, they had lost their bearings and thought they were still over the North Sea when they struck Cheviot. It was later discovered that two of the crew had died on impact and the remaining three had been thrown from the wreckage and, in a bid to escape the machine gun ammunition that was exploding, they had headed down the hillside. Fortunately they had gone down the back of the hill, away from the deep gullies, and found aid at another shepherd's cottage.

Sheila was allowed to warm herself by the kitchen fire till the ambulance arrived, during which time the airmen made a great fuss of her. John Dagg said later that she had enjoyed this much more than the Dickin animal bravery medal she was subsequently awarded. John, however, was very proud of the award and the letter he received from the commander of U.S. Eighth Air Force.

If it had not been for a very brave shepherd and his little dog, four young American airmen would certainly have died that night. John Dagg had realised that if anyone had survived the crash, they would not then have lived through such a blizzard and he decided he could not afford to wait for the storm to pass before initiating a search. John was fully aware that he could have died that night, as shepherds had died on the hill in the past in spite of their detailed knowledge of the land. John Dagg was a special man but Frank Moscrop showed equal courage and compassion by also going to the aid of those in need in such life-threatening circumstances. Sheila's presence on the hill showed formidable courage: she too, was suffering from the cold and would have preferred to be warm at home, but her loyalty to her master made her persevere at his side. Sheila's courage brought her a short burst of nationwide fame but it soon died away, so it is right that the heroic actions of this brave shepherd and his dog are recorded to inspire others.

★★★★★

A sheepdog can also achieve fame by winning an international sheepdog trial, but this is by no means an easy thing to do as dogs which win this accolade must be the cream of the crop in intelligence and sheep-handling skills. However, once secured, such fame lives on in the shepherds' world for many generations, long after the dog has died, as its offspring which will be greatly sought-after for those qualities displayed on the trials field. These champion trial dogs are also working sheepdogs.

One such famous dog around the 1900s was Auld Kep, twice winner of the International Cup, and the property of a very proud Mr James Scott of Ancrum.

Avid spectators at a sheepdog trial in the 1930s.

The following report, written by the famous sheepdog writer Ralph Flesh, shows why this little dog was justifiably famous in the shepherds' world:

Auld Kep — for this is now his familiar name — the winner for the second time of the International Cup, is an average-sized dog of the type of the old Border Collie. He is finely coupled and in action shows to great advantage at the sheepdog trials. When he leaves his master to take command, there is an ease and confidence revealed that instantly stop the flow of speculations. The sheep seem at once to recognize his kindly powers and instead of rebelling, comply with his every request. Having an extremely strong eye he at close quarters throws a mesmeric influence over both sheep and spectators.

Now well-accustomed to the trial course he keeps perfectly cool, carefully scans the ground before beginning and then lends an attentive ear to his master and to his master only no matter the excitement and noise beyond. When scarcely a year old he came to Mr. Scott's hands having then a deal to learn. He has won considerably over £200 in prize money besides cups and medals. Today all authorities recognise him as the greatest sheepdog living. That true working blood courses through his veins is shown by the fact that his sons and daughters filled the entire prize list at the last sheepdog trials at Perth on September 18. He is now eight years old.

In 1850 the average wage of a shepherd was £20 and in 1900 Auld Kep had won in excess of £200, a small fortune for the time. This alone would have made him a legend among the shepherds but the power of his eye, described as 'mesmeric' in the report, is what people really admired. The ability to almost hypnotise the sheep with his stare, turning them into docile creatures, was a sight that spectators would remember for the rest of their lives. Even today Auld Kep is not forgotten in the shepherd world.

Such fame can come to the most unlikely-looking dogs, as was the case at a sheepdog championship held in Perth in 1909. The holder of the championship was David Garlow with his well-known sheep dog, old Venture. A conversation held between this experienced competitor and another Pentland-based shepherd shows how nervous Davie was coming up to the great day.

"Heard the news, Davie?"

"What news?"

"About the championship next week."

"Well, what new terror is threatening us now?"

"The great Suffolk dog is booked and so is the Irish champion and I had an inklin' from Master Whinny, the secretary, the other day that the dog that won the £100 and the Colonial Cup in New Zealand two months since is on the water, bound for the championship at Perth on Wednesday."

Old Hemp, 1893-1901, was the most famous trial dog of all time. She was the bitch from which countless international trial sheepdog champions came: from Moss in 1907 to Jaff II in 1935. Other international champions who came through her line included Old Kep (1908), Sweep (1910&12), Glen (1926), Lad (1913), Haig (1921), Spot (1923), Craig (1930) and many more.

"Indeed, Samuel, indeed! No doubt it will be a stiff struggle but I'm not going to take fright at the tootlin' of a few trumpets. Old Venture has met the best in his time and the poor old chap, though not as glossy and bouncy as he once was, will lower the tails of a few of them yet."

So talked the two shepherds about the much anticipated event. Venture was a famous Collie whose record at both national and international championships had not been broken. While the two men continued in their discussion, Venture slept contentedly by the fireside with one ear raised, ready to receive instructions.

"He's dreaming," remarked Davie, "For after a hard day's work the peace of the body is seldom followed by the perfect peace of the mind."

Davie had perfect confidence in the prowess of Venture but he anticipated an exceptional challenge at the championship the following Wednesday.

The day drew nearer and Davie seemed to be showing some uncharacteristic signs of anxiety. No doubt this was fuelled by Mr. Blacklock Garston boasting that he had produced a dog that would set a higher standard than anything ever before achieved. Come the day of the trials, the quality of the competition had obviously been playing on Davie's mind and his strained nerves had been sensed by Venture.

As the sun rose, the mist dispersed, revealing the stern features of the towering hills surrounding the city of Perth. Shepherds and their families made their way down the glens towards the trial course. Families met up, friendships were renewed and strengthened.

Among the vast crowds there were also many who had no connection with shepherding but simply took great delight in watching the dogs at work. The more knowledgeable among the crowd, of course, had their own particular favourite based on form but also personal preference.

"Davie and old Venture will hold the cup," argued one man, "Wait till you see him at his out-run and then at his shed. If the old chap is in form, nothing will touch him."

"But what about the great Suffolk dog and the one from New Zealand?" questioned another, "I'm fearing that Davie and Venture will have a stiffer job than they have ever had before."

"I saw Venture on the hill separate two lambs from their mother and held them apart like a seven-wired fence. I'm telling you, that dog will keep the cup."

Such discussions, some of them becoming heated, could be found going on in every corner of the trial ground as the audience anticipated the day's event and their excitement grew. In one corner, Mr Garston with the dog that he boasted would reach new heights of excellence, was talking with an old shepherd he had not seen for many months.

"Old Venture is a great dog," said the old shepherd.

"Maybe he is a great dog but be prepared for a surprise," replied Mr Garston confidently.

"You mean to say that boast you made about having a dog that will eclipse all-comers is true?"

"My friend, something the nearest to old Whaff that you ever saw will take the field today and will take the Cup."

"Never, Mr Garston."

"We will not argue the matter any further; time and talent will tell."

The shepherds gathered together at the entrance gate to the trial field and exchanged friendly greetings. The famous Suffolk dog looked eager and the New Zealand champion arrived. But, at a slight distance from the other shepherds, stood a small, square, kindly-faced man with a dog that looked much the same as his master. The man's manner, and even that of his dog, seemed to indicate a

Scenes from some sheepdog trials in the 1940s.

shyness, making them unwilling to introduce themselves to the other shepherds. Nobody seemed to know who this pair were and the question rippled through the crowd.

"Who's that?"

"Apparently it is Magnus Drever from Orkney, with his dog Ronald," replied one smart young fellow who had consulted the catalogue of the day's events.

"Well, he's come an awful long way for nothing," commented numerous spectators who, from the look of man and dog, dismissed them as potential champions.

The three judges took their places, the director of the course called the first competitor and the championship began. Competitor after competitor took the field but none made much impact on the judges, who marked them poorly. Number 8 was called; David Garlow and Venture, the reigning champions, took their place at the post somewhat nervously. At the first command, Venture hesitated slightly; the nervousness of his master transmitting itself to him. He then took the finest out-run of the day but that hesitation was to cost him a mark off the entire performance. Most of the crowd now believed that Davie had retained the cup for another year and even Davie himself was beginning to feel quite confident.

The New Zealand dog ran next, then the Suffolk. Though both put in a brilliant performance, the cup still lay firmly within Davie's grasp and now only one competitor, No. 17, Magnus and Ronald, remained. The crowd were not very excited as this pair took to the field, feeling the Cup was Davie's and it was a waste of time for this uninspiring-looking dog to run. Davie was not so sure: his skilled shepherd's eye could see the dog had a great spirit and the master a quiet confidence.

At Magnus' command, Ronald sped from the post in a wide, smooth and completely faultless out-run, coming on the sheep with such gentleness that they were not the least disturbed but lifted their heads from grazing and began to move in exactly the right direction. In no time at all, the sheep were at Magnus' feet, still quiet and calm; the firm yet gentle spirit of the dog seeming to have captivated not just the sheep, but the audience, too.

Magnus stepped forward a few paces to effect the shed: the removal of two marked sheep from the flock that have to be held to a given count by the dog before allowing them to return to the flock. At Magnus' command, Ronald darted into the flock like a kingfisher swooping into the water, separated the two marked sheep from the flock without any confusion or disturbance, and then held them firm with nothing more than his confident eye.

"He's done it, by gosh," whispered one member of the crowd to another.

"Not yet, there's still the pen, the undoing of many a good run."

As the men whispered, Magnus was opening the gate into the pen into which the sheep had to be corralled to bring the trial to its conclusion. Sheep hate being driven into an enclosed space which is what makes the pen such a fine test of the combined working ability of the shepherd and his dog. Magnus stood motionless by the gate, allowing his dog to take the full burden of the task; many of the most knowledgeable onlookers felt this was risky but Magnus trusted his dog and Ronald responded. Using the power of his eye combined with steady movement so as not to panic the sheep, he drove them calmly, straight into the pen, in just one and a half minutes.

This display of sheer brilliance had the normally dispassionate crowd rushing onto the course with claps and cheers to praise this unknown competitor from the Orkneys. This unremarkable pair had initially been dismissed by the crowd to whom their quiet and steady teamwork was not immediately apparent. This is still often the case in today's image-obsessed society – the outer appearance is observed and the inner strength and skill is overlooked. In the canine world, dogs are often bred for appearance, to the detriment of their natural abilities, even creating physical problems for them – all in the name of beauty.

CHAPTER SEVEN

Breeds of Sheepdog

You might think that the Border Collie, which is the predominant breed used today to work flocks of sheep in this country, is the only breed suitable for working sheep, but this is far from the case. Many different types of dog have been used in the past, some of which are now extinct, like the Manx sheepdog; others turned into show dogs like the Old English sheepdog. So we shall take a look at a number of these breeds to see how they were used and how puppies were selected from a litter and trained to work sheep.

A dog which most people would recognise is the Old English sheepdog which at one time was known as the Sussex sheepdog. This breed was a particular favourite of the shepherds of the South Downs. Though highly intelligent, the Sussex was never considered the equal of the Border Collie but it felt the heat far less and had a much bolder temperament, not possessing any of the timidity that is seen in Collies. This greater tolerance of the summer heat, despite its thick coat, was one of the reasons it was preferred in southern England, as the Collie soon becomes lethargic in such conditions. My own Collies will do any amount of work in the winter and think nothing of venturing out in temperatures of -10°C but on a hot midsummer day will be found hiding under a tree or behind the barns trying to cool themselves.

The Sussex dog is described as shaggy, with a great deal of woolly hair over the face and eyes, bluish grey and white in colour with a stumpy tail and high intelligence.

The Sussex was also noted for showing great devotion to his master and family to the exclusion of all others. A shepherd by the name of William Aylward, based in Lavant, had a Sussex sheepdog called Nimble. He was most proud of his dog and there was a great rivalry between him and a Scottish shepherd who used a Collie to see whose was the better dog. One sheep-washing day at Lavant, the large flock stubbornly refused to cross the bridge to the pen where they were to be held for washing. Doubtless some of the older ewes remembered why they were there and had no desire to receive a soaking and so they milled about the entrance to the bridge, causing a complete bottle-neck. The dogs were pushing from behind but could not change the situation as the large flock, bunched tightly together, formed an impenetrable barrier that prevented the dogs from getting to the source of the trouble.

"Well," said the Scottish shepherd, "Your dog is no cleverer than mine after all, for neither of them can shift this flock."

"That is because I have not told Nimble to mount up yet," replied Aylward.

The Scottish shepherd, not quite understanding what was meant, watched as the command was given and, to his great surprise and amusement, saw the Sussex, Nimble, jump straight onto the backs of the sheep. Without hesitation he then ran swiftly over the undulating mass of wool till he was at the front of the flock. Once there, he snapped at the sheep's ears and within minutes the entire flock of three hundred sheep had been successfully driven over the bridge and penned. The Scottish shepherd had to acknowledge that on this occasion his dog had been well and truly beaten though he did say that his dog could probably have done the same had he too been trained to mount up!

The Sussex sheepdog.

The Sussex

The Sussex sheepdog evolved over the years into the breed now called the Old English sheepdog and, as can be seen from the old photograph of the Sussex sheepdog taken just over one hundred years ago, the appearance of the dog has not changed much. Today's version of the Old English is somewhat larger and heavier and, over the years, it has lost much of its herding ability, though not its courage or its intelligence.

I recall a story about a pedigree show dog of the Old English breed that was in the garden with its master who had decided to have a bonfire to get rid of a large pile of garden rubbish. The rubbish was a little on the damp side and so the man went to his shed and returned with a can of flammable liquid which he poured over the fire. Instantly the fire leapt into life, the flames racing back up to the can which then exploded in his hand, showering him with burning liquid that ignited his shirt.

The man was now well and truly on fire, so threw himself to the ground and began to roll about in a desperate attempt to extinguish the flames. Suddenly he sensed a weight drop on to him: his Old English sheepdog was smothering the flames! Its dense hairy coat effectively extinguished the flames in moments and undoubtedly saved his master's life.

The Manx

The Manx sheepdog of the Isle of Man was a holding and not a driving dog which meant they were kept at heel by the shepherd's side and, when a particular sheep was wanted, the shepherd would point it out and say in Manx, "Grein yn nane shoh," which means "Seize that one". The dog would seize the sheep behind the neck, throw it down and then hold it still, all without hurting or even bruising the sheep. These dogs were described as being smooth-haired, of various colours and very big and strong. These dogs were superseded in 1860, when many Scottish shepherds went to the island, taking their much more versatile sheepdogs.

The Welsh Collie

My favourite sheepdog of all is the magnificent looking Welsh Collie, which has two sub-divisions: the heading dogs and the driving or barking dogs. To learn a bit about the character of these little-known working sheepdogs, it is best to turn to the writings of Erwyd Howells, obviously a Welshman and an expert on the subject of the Welsh sheepdog, having used them his entire life on the beautiful hills around Aberystwyth. Erwyd says:

The Border Collie has an ingrained instinct to work or herd sheep and approaches its sheep with caution as though stalking its charges and never taking its eye off them and if they feel challenged by the sheep they set, that is lie down, eyeing them. The Welsh dogs on the other hand work in a totally different way to the Border with tails up and ears down and have none of their inhibiting characteristics. They are free agents by comparison, with no eye, in fact they are commonly referred to as loose eyed dogs. One thing that I like about them is that when you have got sheep into the yards they go about their own business whereas the Border Collie will be eyeing the sheep under a gate or through a fence unable to switch off because of their overpowering natural instincts.

When the Welsh dogs are under pressure to move their sheep, they bark and are at their happiest when they are working large flocks of sheep. They have a tremendous amount of energy and work well in hot weather. Many Borders especially if they have a thick coat do not stick heat too well. When there is a large mob of sheep on an open hill you feel with a few Welsh dogs that you can dictate as to where the flock goes because of their strong presence. Many people have handled sheep and dogs all their lives but have no idea of the total cussedness of open mountain sheep or wethers, when they want to escape, especially in rough ground or broken rocks, which give them a big advantage in their intention.

The driving/barking dog was and still is a very important aspect of a hill farm. They were instrumental in keeping sheep boundaries, driving the sheep back into their own sectors(when you look at a hillside and see thousands of sheep, you may think that they all belong to the same flock but that is not the case. There are many flocks and each has its designated place on the hill, to which it must be kept or they will be trespassing on the grazing of another. It is the driving/barking dog left on the hill with the sheep that ensures his flock sticks to its sector and none from another flock encroach onto the sector he is responsible for).

During the summer driving/barking dogs also ensured that the flock did not come down onto the lower slopes, the grazing of which was being preserved for the autumn. Going back long ago before the time of stock-proof boundaries, this type of dog was the only means

The Welsh Collie: now a very rare breed and a worker of the open hillsides

by which hill farms could keep their hay, oats and green crops from the scavenging sheep. These dogs were kept out day and night and as soon as they saw a sheep within a given distance they would drive off the woolly transgressor aggressively.

The driving/barking dogs should not be thought of as a race apart from the heading dog: the difference lies in the training given and the work done, not the actual breed; both kinds of dogs being Welsh sheepdogs, just performing different roles. In fact it was not uncommon for the driving/barking dog after several years to graduate into a heading dog. (The best way to understand the difference between a heading dog and a driving/barking dog is to think of the first as a dog for the fine, more intricate close work and the driving/ barking dog as the one for the coarser tasks.) Welsh sheepdogs can be any colour – black and tan, blue merle, brown, brindle, black and white, grey; and some are black with flecks of white in their coat known as cibwrw eira – a snow storm dog.

Welsh Collie puppies

One trait of the Welsh sheepdog which Erwyd does not mention is its extremely high level of intelligence which many believe to be the equal of the Border Collie. The Welsh sheepdog is a very rare breed today with only a few litters being birthed each year. The dogs are used by a handful of die-hard shepherds who still value this breed for its abilities on the open hill. These shepherds are generally Welshmen who also have a strong desire to keep this piece of Welsh canine history alive and working.

Without such men, the breed would surely be consigned to the realms of history, which would be a great shame: as you can see from photographs in this book, they are a most noble-looking dog, with a real sense of presence and purpose.

Whilst in Wales, it is worth noting a couple of sheepdogs that have now disappeared: the Welsh Hillman and the Welsh Grey, both of which influenced the Welsh sheepdog of today. The Hillman is a dog that can be traced back as far as the 10th century, when it was most likely used by Welsh noblemen as a hunting dog to chase and bring down game, the noblemen following on horseback. So this was a large and powerful creature with a great deal of speed, bravery and tenacity: and somewhere in the past this hunting ability was tempered and redirected to be applied to herding.

The Welsh Grey was a small, very shaky dog, not dissimilar to the Bearded Collie of old. There is not much written about this rough mischievous-looking little dog which looks more like a lurcher than a sheepdog, but what little is recorded clearly asserts that it was very intelligent and rugged. This seems to be a feature of all Welsh dogs; even the Corgi before it was modified by breeders seeking to beautify it.

The Hillman, no longer a working dog today, dates back to 10th century Wales.

The Bearded Collie

The Bearded Collie has been somewhat refined over the years though it has by no means lost its old working instincts, for several shepherds with an interest in the history of sheepdogs have taken modern Bearded Collies and trained them to work with sheep, even getting them up to trials level. In spite of this, the Bearded Collies are not able to outperform the Border Collie which is probably why the old working strain has died out.

Very little is written about the history of the Bearded Collie, but it does appear that this Scottish sheepdog had its origin in dogs purchased for the price of one ewe and a ram from the Polish who sailed to Scotland to trade in sheep in 1514. The Bearded Collie used to be known by various other names depending on the part of Scotland you were in: the names included Highland Collie, Mountain Collie, Scottish Sheepdog and Hairy Mou'ed Collie (Hairy-Mouthed Collie). If you take a look at Tweed in the chapter on sheepdogs at war, you would at first glance consider him an out-and-out hairy mongrel but he is in fact a Highland Sheepdog.

All the names used for this breed clearly show us that it was a dog of the hills and its double coat, which was never groomed so as not to strip away the essential under-hair, was a perfect protection from the severe weather experienced in the Scottish mountains, keeping the dog warm and dry in the mountain mist, which is even more pervasive than rain.

Grooming may make a dog look very fine but too much grooming can strip a dog's coat of its protective qualities. This can also apply to horses and, during the First World War, horses died in their thousands, not just from the hail of shells falling on the battlefield but by succumbing to the elements. Cavalry regulations insisted that horses had to be

The Bearded Collie, timid, but hard-working.

The Welsh Grey: a poor image but a rare one of a now extinct breed.

groomed every day and the grooming took away all the depth from the horses' coats so that in the mud and rain they simply perished. When an order was issued to throw away the grooming kits and to let the horses grow their coats naturally, the war horses fared much better against the elements. The early sheepdogs may look scruffy compared to a show dog today but their untended coats proved perfect protection from the elements.

The old-fashioned Bearded Collie was a highly intelligent animal but it was rather timid, needing a very patient and loving trainer to get the best out of it. However, when correctly trained, these dogs were very committed to their work. It is interesting to note the marked similarity between the Bearded Collie working on the Scottish hills and the Welsh Grey working on the Welsh hills, suggesting a shared ancestry.

The Border Collie

The most famous of all sheepdog breeds the world over is clearly the Border Collie, its fame being due to its extreme level of intelligence and its ability to use its eye to control sheep, an ability unique to the Border Collie amongst the sheep dogs of the British Isles. 'Using its eye to control sheep' does not mean that the Collie has the ability to hypnotise the sheep it is handling but that the Collie is able to transmit its intentions through its eye.

The Border Collie is a breed that has its roots in the border country of Scotland, a region of much fighting and cross-border raiding. In the past, dogs were more than likely used to steal sheep and cattle from across the border so it is not surprising that a dog from that area is intelligent and cunning, for this is often the case where dogs are used by man in any kind of illegal activity. The lurcher, which was

The Border Collie - the most famous of all the sheepdog breeds.

The Border Collie approaches his sheep with caution as though stalking them, with his eyes fixed on the sheep and his body close to the ground. Note that the tail is down and ears pricked whilst working.

The Collie is one of the most intelligent and lively of breeds, always looking at his master, awaiting the next instruction.

used by gypsies to great effect for taking rabbits in order to feed the family is another example of a very intelligent dog that was much favoured by Colonel Richardson who trained the messenger dogs during the First World War.

Another unique feature of the Border Collie, not seen in other British sheepdogs, is the way it works with its belly and chest near to the ground, with its legs beneath it like coiled-up springs, when it is working close to the sheep. This creeping position allows the dog to dart about rapidly and out-manoeuvre the sheep.

It is the use of the eye, the creeping movement and the extreme level of intelligence that have made the Border Collie the number one sheepdog in the world, and rightly so. Most people think that the Border Collie is always black and white but, though this is by far the predominant colour, they are also tricolour and blue or red merles which, in my opinion, are the most striking of all the Border Collie colours.

Every shepherd will keep at least two dogs, but usually three or four, to cover such things as injury, bitches on heat and the nursing of pups. Where the shepherd needs to control large areas of hillside, several dogs are required to work together in order to bring in very large flocks of sheep.

Sheepdog training

For the first four or five months of a puppy's life, there was very little in the way of training and, before there was traffic around in the countryside, and when it was safe to do so, pups were allowed free rein in order to explore and gain confidence. The farm children were also encouraged - though I suspect they took very little encouragement - to play with the pups, as close human contact was considered an essential part of the puppy's development.

Training with sheep would begin in a small enclosed paddock with no more than seven or eight sheep. Initially the pup would simply be allowed to chase the sheep, then the shepherd would begin to curtail the pup's enthusiasm and thus the training begins.

Voice commands are the starting point, later replaced by a whistle, for the simple reason that a whistle travels further on the hill than the human voice. The dog must learn to lie down, which is basically the 'stop' command and once issued the dog is expected to lie still until another command is given.

Next it must learn to go to the left or the right as required: a common command for a movement to the right is 'Come Bye' and for the left, 'Away Here' (with regional variations). A popular way of teaching these commands was to tie (couple) the pup to a fully trained Collie that would then act as teacher, sending the trainee left or right as commanded. It is surprising how quickly the youngster learns to associate the command with the required turn and so can be unfastened from the teacher dog very soon.

Another command that the trainee must learn is 'Come On,' a call to move towards the sheep and this again used to be taught by attaching the youngster to a teaching dog.

These are the four basic commands which the shepherd employs to get a dog to gather and work the sheep. There are, of course, more detailed commands that will enable the dog to carry out a larger range of tasks but the initial four commands are the foundation on which all is built and these must be fully mastered before further work is done.

Once the dog is fully trained to the voice, the whistle is then introduced in conjunction with the voice commands and the highly intelligent Collie very quickly learns what the whistle means. To many onlookers, the use of the whistle seems to be some kind of magic but it is simply a system of

It was about 30 years ago that I first saw a lithe Collie on a dairy farm disappear on its belly into a small copse appearing moments later proudly carrying a rabbit in its mouth. Before the arrival of myxomatosis, when the rabbit population was considerably larger, Collies (during their off-duty moments) often caught rabbits to provide meat for the shepherd's table – the dog happily accepting the entrails, head and feet as its reward. My Collies have had their hunting instincts very much encouraged, making them most effective in the field.

coded messages. For example, two long notes may be used to turn the dog right and four short notes to turn it left, the actual code varying from shepherd to shepherd.

Breeding and Selecting Pups

Many shepherds breed their own sheepdogs, using a neighbour's dog over their own bitch, to prevent in-breeding.

The Border Collie litter from which my own Collies came.

Left: I chose the second and third from the left. Both had black roofs to their mouths and caught my eye.
Right: My pups as fine adult Collies. I obviously chose well.

Other shepherds will buy their dogs from proven blood-lines. When it came to choosing pups, shepherds had many little tricks for selecting the best ones from a litter. It is a very important matter, for it has a tremendous impact on the shepherd's ability to do his job. Choosing a pup that turned out to be a poor worker would be a waste of the shepherd's valuable time in training it and would provide him with a work companion that was not able to carry its load.

Many shepherds insisted on selecting a pup with a black roof to its mouth, in the belief that this was the sign of a good worker. Others would remove all the pups from the bitch and place them a short distance away from her. The first pup that she retrieved would be the one that they selected.

Some shepherds liked to select the runt of the litter and I must admit that I often do the same. Quite surprisingly, these often turn out to be the most phenomenal workers. Many avoided red pups which could be mistaken on the open hills for foxes. Certain shepherds would choose a pup with dew claws and others would chose a pup without.

A favourite way of choosing a puppy was to select the first one to come and introduce itself, indicating a level of confidence and boldness. The plain fact is that very few sheep-dogs turn out to be poor workers, most having the ability to perform the job to a level of proficiency for everyday work. It is only when it comes to the selection of a trials dog that one has to delve really deeply into the pedigree of the animal, otherwise, with very few exceptions, any Collie that is loved and carefully trained will do its duty well enough.

It is amazing that the sheepdog can be traced back to the tenth century and yet it is still as important to the hill shepherd one thousand years later. Despite all the huge technological advances in agriculture that have seen the demise of the working horse, there is nothing that can take the place of the working sheepdog.

CHAPTER EIGHT

The Shepherd's Winter

Winter is the shepherd's greatest enemy, especially in previous centuries when each year shepherds and their sheep perished as they faced the coldest of weather and all the fury that nature can muster. According to records, winters used to be much more severe than those experienced these days. For example, in the period 1500 to 1850 the Thames froze fifteen times, with such a thick sheet of ice forming on the water that fairs were held on the river. The last Thames fair was held in 1814, a particularly cruel winter. Also in the winter of 1814, a pig slaughtered on a farm in Wales froze solid overnight and remained frozen for a full thirteen weeks, and another account that year states that a loaf of bread in a farm kitchen froze to such an extent that next morning it had to be cut with an axe before it could be toasted for breakfast.

The winter of 1772-73 was particularly harsh and a sheep farmer by the name of William Williams of Dolgoch, Wales, who had a flock of some 24,000 sheep, lost half his flock, a staggering 12,000 sheep, over a period of about four months. A loss on this enormous scale must have been absolutely soul-destroying; going out day after day to find more of your animals buried, smothered, starving or freezing; the cruel fist of winter killing slowly and painfully. Trying to fight an enemy with such might requires a huge amount of determination and stamina of the shepherd in both mind and body, in conditions that would sap the energies of the toughest.

On a hill farm called Cae Coch a momentous snowstorm hit in the winter of 1823, with such vengeance that this single storm took 700 ewes in one night from a flock of 1200.

In 1895, in the area around Devil's Bridge in Wales, the temperature dropped to a staggering 34 degrees below freezing – the kind of temperature you expect in Alaska. It is amazing that anything survived that winter, for sheep are just not designed to cope with those kinds of temperatures. That same winter, on a hill farm called Dolwen, 1,600 sheep perished of the cold and were skinned, the carcasses being used for meat and the skins saved to cure. Even when nature brings disaster, the shepherd does what he can to salvage the situation, allowing nothing to go to waste.

It is calculated that today one third of all the food that goes into a kitchen ends up being thrown away but in the past such an extravagance would not only have been frowned upon as a waste of God-given resources but it could also

The decimation of sheep flocks brought about by the cruel winter of 1947.

have meant total ruin. This is why everything that could be salvaged and used, was salvaged and used despite the tremendous amount of work that this involved. Many traditional dishes, such as haggis, came about as a result of the need to use every available scrap of an animal.

★★★★★

One of the more recent severe winters, still within living memory, is the winter of 1947 when approximately 3,000,000 sheep perished and a disaster fund was set up to help farmers recover. In May 1947 the fund stood at a staggering £240,000 but sadly the money did not come quickly enough for some sheep farmers who took their own lives, feeling that the winter had ruined them and their way of life. Generally shepherds are extremely stoical individuals who, with faith, hope and the help of their Collie dog, struggle through every obstacle to make something out of the situation but occasionally their spirit is fractured beyond repair and they sink into a depression from which there is no escape.

Sheep can cope with a great deal of bad weather, which they combat by moving to lower ground, when they sense the approach of a storm, where the snowfall will be less and the temperatures slightly less brutal. When snow has covered the ground, the sheep dig through the snow to access the grass beneath. A real problem arises when the snow is so deep or so frozen that the grass cannot be reached and, if this pitiful situation remains for a long period of time, then the sheep lose condition rapidly through starvation, are unable to maintain their body heat and simply perish.

Being buried alive for a few days, as often happens in snow drifts, is not necessarily a death sentence to sheep, as there is usually an air pocket around them, sufficient to keep them alive for some considerable time. The snow which has buried the sheep effectively forms a blanket which provides surprisingly good insulation and keeps the sheep warm no matter how low the temperature drops. Erwyd Howells records the following incident of a sheep being buried in a drift in the 1981/82 storm:

A neighbour John Watkin had sheep buried in the shelter of a hedge and a while later I found a ewe on Lluest-y-rhos land that had been under a drift of snow for eighteen days. She had eaten the grass and lichen around her to the roots and also a bit of the wool from her sides. Apart from being a bit thin she was perky and ran away to join her mates. Ironically sheep that have been imprisoned thus for a while, after being rescued and let out of what was a warm place, are sometimes susceptible to pneumonia and can die as a result.

One ewe was buried for three weeks in a snowdrift in the storm of 1937 and survived with a little tender care from the shepherd. The following reports in the *Scotsman*

A shepherd digging out a ewe that his dog discovered buried in the deep snow.

newspaper give quite a graphic illustration of the storms of 1937 and their effect on the shepherd.

March 1st 1937

The wettest February for seventy-one years ended last night with a blizzard, which raged from the North of Scotland to the South Coast and from Ireland to the Eastern Counties of England. Thousands of square miles of countryside were covered by snow with drifts many feet deep. Villages were completely cut off, cars and buses and trains had to be abandoned, road traffic was disorganized and trains were seriously delayed.

March 9th 1937

SHEEP PERISH IN STORM
– Nearly 300 Ewes Lost on a Border Farm Buried in Snow

The snowstorm has taken a heavy toll of sheep in Lauderdale, Berwickshire. On the farm of Blythe near Lauder tenanted by Captain A. R. McDougal about 140 half-bred ewes and about 50 black-faced ewes are dead and about 90 black-faced ewes are missing. It is presumed that these are also dead and carcases are being recovered daily. Blythe is an exposed farm with but little shelter. The storm came on during the night and the damage was done before morning. Sheep retreated before the wind into hollows where they were quickly snowed under. There was fifteen feet of snow in some of these hollows. Many animals perished on clear ground. The wind was the fiercest experienced for years and as the half-bred ewes were within a week or two of lambing they were not in a condition to withstand such conditions. A number of ewes which escaped from the storm are now dying from the effects of it. Although losses in these parts have been frequent in the past, none has been so heavy. Few farmers in the Borders have escaped without losses, scores of lambs meeting their deaths in the storms.

My Border cross Welsh Collie will happily go out in deep snow and temperatures of −10°c to −15°c do not deter him in the least. I have known Collies to sleep outside in the snow, becoming completely covered overnight and staying warm, much like huskies in the arctic actually, insulated by the blanket of snow over them.

The story of a shepherd by the name of James M Wilson farming on the Borders at the time of this epic blizzard is well worth reading as it describes the amount of gut-wrenching physical effort and sheer determination that goes into caring for a flock that has been caught by the fast-moving drift snow. Mr Wilson knew that a blizzard was coming because he noticed that his sheep were moving down from the high ground to take shelter behind the woodlands; a sure sign that the weather was going to change though the skies above gave no indication of it. The flock was gathered in its entirety; 900 ewes lay still and quiet, waiting for the onslaught, in this sheltered spot roughly two miles from the farm.

That night the snow came like it had never come before in living memory, a deluge of fat snowflakes hurtling from the heavens in a great rush to cover the ground, driven horizontally by a wind like nothing ever before seen. The snow only lasted for one day but the hurricane wind would not cease; whipping up the light fluffy snow and piling it into huge mountainous drifts.

When Mr Wilson went to check on his flock, he found that at least half the ewes had disappeared beneath the drifts but he was not too worried, knowing that sheep can survive a considerable time beneath the snow. He had brought a shovel and his dogs obligingly pointed out the spot in which he needed to dig and so the task of freeing the sheep from their snowy prison began. Despite the severe cold and the biting wind, the shepherd was soon sweating heavily as he shifted tons of snow to recover his flock.

To his great delight he had not lost a single ewe. In order for the sheep to stay alive they needed food to combat

the conditions; this had to be carried two miles by hand, bales of hay and bags of hard feed. Hauling all the necessary provisions to keep the sheep alive was a monumental task for one man, going back and forth all day and still there was only just enough food to keep the flock alive. Despite his most valiant efforts, shepherd Wilson just could not keep this supply line running as the physical demands of the task were

This wether, rescued from a snow drift after three weeks, was soon nursed back to health.

wearing him down and the hurricane winds creating huge drifts of snow showed no signs of abating.

Shepherd Wilson decided that there was only one thing to do; if he could not get the food to the sheep then the sheep must be got to the food. So he took three Collies out to the sheep: Nell, Craig and Roy. Nell was used to separate ten sheep from the main flock, which shepherd Wilson intended to use like a snowplough driving through the snow, making a path that the others could follow.

He realized that the sheep would need a little help in this so he took a shovel and began to clear a narrow path that the sheep would be able to widen. He gave Nell one word of command then began to dig. For the entire course of the two mile journey back to the farm, Nell did not require any further command but knew exactly what was expected of her. When her master had cleared ten to twelve feet of snow, she moved the sheep forward and they consolidated the track before the winds had time to obliterate it.

Then the remainder of the flock, under the charge of Craig and Roy working as a brace, came on closely behind Nell. Thus a slow-moving train of ewes, guided by the dogs, moved snail-like through the deep snow. Frequent breaks were required for the shepherd and the sheep to take a rest.

After a tense five and a half hours, the mammoth task was accomplished through the strength and endurance of the shepherd and his dogs, working as a tight-knit unit, each having its part in the proceedings which they played to perfection. Shepherd Wilson is not the only one who would have acted in this heroic fashion: he is but one example of what would have been happening all over the country as shepherds demonstrated true grit and determination in protecting their flock from the grip of winter's deadly embrace.

CHAPTER NINE

Strange Tales

THERE ARE stories told about the feats performed by sheepdogs, mostly Collies, that almost defy belief: actions that would suggest a level of understanding, deduction and planning that one would normally assume to be beyond the abilities of a dog. I am not trying to intimate that dogs have human characteristics but simply to suggest that they can have much greater intellectual powers than is generally recognized.

I shall begin with the story of Tom Morgan's dog. Tom was a travelling shepherd and was said to have a marvellous way with all animals, a bit like a shepherding version of St Francis of Assisi. Erwyd Howells recalls a story about this gifted shepherd in his book *Good Men And True* as follows:

One day Tom Morgan was on his way to Aber-gwngu where they were dipping and the farm dogs ran out at the sight of a strange dog approaching and Tom's dog got stuck into them, felling them left and right. Tom came onto the scene of the battle and spoke to his dog;

"Well, well, you've come all the way to Aber-gwngu and the first thing you do is quarrel with these little dogs." And his dog sank lower and lower with each word, as if in shame. "Now then, to show that you are sorry, jump into that cart and sing for the people" and jump into the cart he did and started howling in earnest.

Tom was invited in for a meal and his horse was put in the stable. After the meal Tom was ready to set off and asked a nearby lad to open the stable door but not to touch the horse. The door duly opened, Tom gave a whistle and the horse made a beeline for him.

On another occasion, he had asked the dog to sing for old Mr J.E. Raw at Ty-llwyd and the dog duly went about his piece with gusto but Tom told him "Mr Raw doesn't like loud singing — a little quieter please." And the dog obliged in a lower tone.

The way that Tom's dog was able to interpret his master's meaning suggests that he could understand sufficient specific words to work out what was required of him. This ability to understand complex language can be further demonstrated by a remarkable event recorded by James Hogg, a shepherd and a writer in the 1800s whose poetry is still well read today in Scotland. He wrote the following about his dog Hector:

Mention the word 'rabbit' to Pilot my Collie cross and his eyes brighten and his body fills with excitement for he knows the meaning of the word as he looks to me to point out the location of the rabbit.

It can not be supposed that Hector could understand all that was passing in the little family circle but he certainly comprehended a good part of it. In particular it was very easy to discover that he rarely missed aught that was said about himself, the sheep, the cat or of a hunt. When aught of that nature came to be discussed, Hector's attention and impatience soon became manifest. There was one winter evening I said to my mother that I was going to Bowerhope for a fortnight for that I had more conveniency for writing with Alexander Laidlaw than at home and I added "But I will not take Hector with me for he is constantly quarrelling with the rest of the dogs, singing music or breeding some uproar." "No," quoth she, "Leave Hector with me; I like to have the beast at hame, poor fallow."

These were all the words that passed. The next morning the waters were in great flood and I did not go away till after breakfast; but when the time came for tying up Hector, he was wanting.

"Where the deuce's is that beast?" said I. "I will wager that he heard what we were saying yesternight and has gone off for Bowerhope as soon as the door was opened this morning."

"If that be the case I'll think the beast most canny," said my mother.

The Yarrow was so large as to be quite impassable so that I had to go up by St. Mary's Loch and go across by the boat and on drawing near to Bowerhope I soon perceived that matters had gone precisely as I suspected. Hector had made his escape early in the morning, had swam the river and was sitting "like a drookit hen," on a knoll at the east end of the house awaiting my arrival with much impatience. I had great attachment to this animal.

The fact that Hector knew when to make his escape and when his master would arrive for his visit at Bowerhope is quite remarkable as it demonstrates not just the ability to understand a good number of words but the ability to put them into the context of a time frame; Hector not just understanding the word 'tomorrow' but when tomorrow was. Hector was also able to associate words with locations for he knew which farm was being discussed. Had Hector simply followed his master, that would have been less remarkable but for him to go on ahead shows a very developed level of understanding, reasoning and planning which most people do not ascribe to dogs.

The Sheepdog who could Count

There are even records of shepherd dogs that are able to count, one such being a dog belonging to a Welsh shepherd. This shepherd believed he had twenty-five ewes corralled in a paddock but, just to make sure, he sent his dog ahead, telling it to "Go count the sheep." Moments later the dog returned and the shepherd began counting, "One – two – three..." Each time the shepherd said a number, the dog would issue a single bark. When the shepherd reached twenty-four the dog barked but then came twenty-five and the dog stayed silent. The shepherd repeated 'twenty-five' and still the dog stayed silent.

Being convinced that he had twenty-five ewes in the paddock, the shepherd once more said 'twenty-five,' this time with even more conviction; but nothing would induce the dog to bark. Somewhat annoyed, the shepherd went into the paddock and counted the ewes for himself. Sure enough, there were only twenty-four; one had escaped. The twenty-fives ewes did not comprise the whole flock so the dog was used to working with different numbers of animals according to what job the shepherd was intending to perform. So this dog really did know there was a ewe missing from the paddock and would not change his mind.

Not only does the Collie seem to have the ability to understand language, it also demonstrates a coherent and logical mind. James Hogg wrote concerning the reasoning faculties of sheepdogs:

'I have hardly ever seen a shepherd's dog do anything without perceiving his reasons for it. I have often amused myself in calculating what his motives were for such and such things and I generally found them very cogent ones.'

Hogg's family was a very religious one, as was the norm in his day amongst shepherds, and each evening prayers would be said around the table in the farmhouse. It was Hogg's father who led the prayers and each evening without fail, just seconds before the conclusion, Hogg's dog, Hector, would jump to his feet and dash about the room barking loudly, as if adding his 'Amen'. This greatly perplexed James Hogg, for how on earth did Hector know when the prayers were going to end? They were not of a formal nature, the words were not the same each time and there was no fixed duration, yet Hector never failed to know when the end was approaching. This seems to suggest that the dog was reading people on a level other than their words or actions. Just as a dog can smell much more than we can, perhaps he can also perceive more, in a way that we once knew, but have since lost.

The Dog and the Baker

Another interesting story relates again to a Collie, this time in America, although I do not know for certain that this dog belonged to a shepherd. The owner of this dog had trained his loyal companion to take a sum of money to a bakery where the baker, expecting the dog, would give him a bag of sweet biscuits which were his master's favourites. The dog would then return to his master with the contents of the package untouched.

One day the man, finding that he had no money to hand, wrote an I.O.U. addressed to the baker and the dog took this instead. The baker accepted the I.O.U. and gave the dog the usual package. The man found this system to be more convenient and so he continued the practise but when he went in to the bakers to settle the bill, he found it to be in excess of the biscuits he had consumed. As the baker and the man argued about it, the dog appeared and promptly handed a sheet of folded paper to the baker which, upon inspection, was completely blank. After receiving the first few I.O.U.s, the baker knew what the order was to be and so simply completed the order and threw the sheet of paper away unread. The quick-witted dog had linked the sheet of paper with the biscuits and, whenever it felt in need of a snack, had taken a sheet of paper and delivered it to the baker, then eaten the biscuits on the way home. The level of reasoning involved in this rather cunning act is the kind you would expect to see in a small child, not a dog.

The following two stories show us that the dog is often operating on a different level of awareness to human beings. In 1923 a girl was walking along a road and did not hear a bus approaching behind her. The driver had not seen the girl either and, just as the bus was about to smash into her, the girl's Collie pushed her violently to one side. This valiant dog had sensed the danger seconds before it struck and was able to save his charge although he himself was run over. The girl had walked down this lane many times before with her dog and buses had passed them safely so how did the Collie know that this time was different?

In a similar vein, a child of just three was out alone one day, having escaped from a garden and was understand-ably at that age oblivious to surrounding danger. She was just about to step off a pavement into the path of a car when Bob, a sheepdog, suddenly appeared and grabbed the child by her clothing, pulling her back from the kerbside and thus saving the little girl's life. The level of reasoning required to assess the potential danger and act on it shows a remark-

In certain areas the sheepdog has a much higher level of aware-ness than a human, a fact identified long ago by the Swiss army. They made use of this awareness in the German Shepherd dog for mountain rescue operations in the Alps. In more recent times the sheepdog's deep awareness through its acute senses has been used in earthquake zones where such breeds as the Collie and the German Shepherd have been used to rescue victims from the rubble after an earthquake.

able degree of deduction and an instinctive concern for the welfare of a small child. The dog did not know this child and yet reacted promptly to save her. I have mentioned before that the sheepdog was often expected to look after small children on the farm where he lived and I wonder whether this was the case with Bob.

A Sense of Life

When the ship *Formidable* sank in 1915 off the south coast of England, reports stated that the captain of the ship was observed standing on the bridge smoking calmly with his terrier at his side. As the ship tipped, the pair, who had loved one another in life, remained together as they slipped beneath the waves and drowned.

Some of the crew however were rescued and were taken to a nearby inn where they received medical attention. One man, despite everyone's best efforts to resuscitate him, did not respond and was left for dead. However, Lassie, a local Collie, did not believe the man to be dead and went and lay beside him to give him warmth, and licked his face vigorously. Eventually, he made a slight moan and Lassie barked wildly to alert the doctor and bring him back. The astonished doctor made further efforts to resuscitate him and the man left for dead was brought back to life. Had Lassie not sensed the life still lingering in this man, he would certainly have died that day.

Sheepdogs, in fact all breeds of dogs, have a depth to them that has not yet been fully recognized, which is why there are so many records of extraordinary deeds being carried out by dogs that are beyond explanation. At the beginning of the twentieth century, the head of the New York veterinary college, Dr. S.K. Johnston said; "In my opinion the dog is only beginning to have its day."

Like the old shepherds, he saw a depth in our canine friends that is beyond reasoning and maybe, one day, we will realize a dog's full potential. Some advances have been made, for example, by the army using dogs to save lives by the detection of explosive devices, but there are those with even greater aspirations, hoping to use dogs to identify disease in human beings, with some already skilled in scenting out certain cancers. There is great scepticism in certain areas of the medical profession over such an approach but, if Man could learn to trust the abilities of the dog, not just its powerful nose but its intelligence, motivation and love, like Dr Johnston, I believe that the dog could have an even greater impact on humanity than it has to date.

I spend much of my time in the company of intelligent dogs and, like Dr Johnston, I believe there are greater depths to the dogs abilities than have yet been discovered.

CHAPTER TEN

Drovers and their Dogs

TODAY, when sheep or cattle are moved from farms to stock auctions, it is done by motor transport but this would previously have been done by drovers. These hardy, respected, honest men took charge of large flocks of sheep or herds of cattle which they would drive sometimes hundreds of miles to such locations as Smithfield market in London, to sell them. They would then return to the farmer with the money from the deal and the commission they would receive from this made them wealthy men.

This was not suitable work for the weak as great distances had to be covered on foot over rough terrain and in all weathers. They were also responsible for large sums of money to pay tolls on the many bridges along the way. They were in charge of possibly thousands of sheep or hundreds of cattle worth a small fortune and, of course, the loss of any stock would mean a loss of income to the farmer who had entrusted them to the drover. The work of the drover was also dangerous as highwaymen were the scourge of the remote roads and they knew that the drover provided rich pickings.

To get an idea of what the drover did and what he looked like, we can take a look at a piece from *The Gentleman's Magazine* written in 1797:

"Having rambled to the junction of the two roads upon Chalk Hill on the sultry morning of July 24 1797 I rested until a boy trudging and singing at a great rate came up to me. I suppose you are deciding which way to take, he enquired. Travelling the same way we set off together and I found my companion a most famous little chatterer,

*not much above three feet high and fifteen years of age. He told me
he had been to Smithfield with some sheep; that he went every week
and had thirty miles to walk before night.*

*His frock was compactly bound up and tied across his shoul-
ders. The straps of his shoes formed a studied cross below the buckles
which he took care to tell me had cost him nine pence in London the
Saturday before. Turnpike tickets were stuck in his hatband noticing
the number of sheep he had paid for and the lash of his whip was
twisted round the handle, which he converted into a walking stick.*

*I soon found, though so small a being, he was a character of no
little consequence upon the road and he told me any returning chaise
or tax-cart would give him a lift for nothing. He was familiar with
every one we passed.*

*He wanted no hints to make him loquacious and thus his
busy mind unfolded itself: Now sir do you know I have a very good
master and he promises if I behave well to make a man of me. When
I went to live with him I was a poor, ragged, half-starved parish
boy without father or mother, or never had any as I know of. I have
now two better coats than this (which by the by was all one complete
shred of darn and patch-work) and I have a spick and span new hat
I never had on but Whit-Sunday last and I am to learn too (proudly
stretching himself and brushing up his eyebrows), my master says, to
write; but he has told me so, such a mortal while, I fear he will forget
it. I asked him if he could read. Aye, in the Testament. I have almost
finished the Gospel according to St John and I can repeat the Lord's
Prayer and Belief too — the latter of which he ran over as quick as
possible and asked me if he had missed a word.*

*The naïve simplicity with which he delivered himself made
him rise rapidly in my good opinion and as we paced on he repaid
every nod he received with manifold interest. On parting as I was
turning a corner which took me out of sight he shrilled out God bless
you."*

This drove in the 1940s gives some sense of the much bigger droves that occurred in the 1800s. Droves were seen as late as the 1960s in rural areas where sheep were taken locally to markets or railheads. It was the lorry that brought droving to an end.

This young fellow was certainly a large character and that seems to be a feature of the drover, his travelling endowing him with a gregarious nature.

Another feature seemingly common to all drovers and shared with shepherds was their faith, and they were respected church-goers. This was to be expected as a farmer would surely entrust his sheep or cattle only to a man whose integrity was well-known. Some writers paint the drover as a roguish character with a fondness for taverns but this cannot have been entirely the case as they had to inspire the trust of others in dealing with large sums of money and livestock. It was mentioned that the boy's hat band was full of tickets for the numerous toll bridges that he had crossed, for which he would have had to pay large sums of money. This boy of only fifteen years had inspired sufficient confidence in him to be trusted with a purse of some considerable value.

The strong Welsh Collie was a popular dog amongst drovers for the driving of both sheep and cattle.

If the shepherd was a quiet man of the hills, the drover was a bold man of the highways. However, no matter how skilled the drover, he could not have moved a flock or herd without the assistance of his dog, The drover's dog shared some similarities but was not the same as the shepherd's dog. This article, that appeared in *Pictorial Half Hours* in 1851, gives some idea of what a drover's dog might have looked like.

"This useful animal is larger than the shepherd's dog, the hair is generally shorter and the tail even when not cut purposely often appears as if it had been so. Berwick, who was well acquainted with the drovers and the shepherd's dog, speaking of the former says; Many are whelped with short tails, which seem as if they had been cut and these are called in the north self-tailed dogs. The same writer is disposed to consider this breed as a true or permanent kind and he informs us that great attention is paid to it.

It seems to us however that the drover's dog is in reality a cross between a shepherd's dog and some other race, perhaps the terrier. It often partakes largely of the character of the shepherd's dog but is taller in the limbs. These dogs are singularly quick and prompt in their actions and as all who have watched them in the crowded, noisy, tumultuous assemblage of men and beasts in Smithfield must have observed, they are both courageous and intelligent. To their masters, who often ill-treat them (the drover has not always the kind heart of the shepherd) they are faithful and attached.

The term 'cut tail' is what we call today a docked tail and the kind of dog referred to here is similar to that pictured in the photo at the opening of this chapter. This excerpt implies the drover is unkind to his dogs but this could not always have been the case as they also inspired great loyalty. Many accounts exist of drovers being attacked by highwaymen and the drover's dogs, without command, would charge into the fight to rescue their masters from gangs of men armed with swords and flint-lock pistols, so it was not uncommon for the dogs to be badly injured. The drover could not, of course, abandon the flock or herd in his charge so he had to pay someone to tend to his dog, and he would continue on his journey and retrieve his dog at a later date.

The following article written in 1853 by James Jesse shows us a little of how the drover's dog worked.

"I was interested the other day in watching a flock of sheep attended by a drover and his dog as they were passing along a turnpike road. The man went into an inn by the roadside leaving his dog to look after the sheep. They spread themselves over the road and footpath, some lying down and others feeding while the dog faithful to his trust watched them carefully.

When any carriage passed along the road or a person was seen on the footpath the dog gently drove the sheep on one side to make a passage and then resumed his station near the inn door. Those indeed who have travelled much at the time of the great fair of Weyhill must have observed the sagacity of the drover's dogs on the approach of a carriage. A passage is made for it through the most numerous flocks of sheep in the readiest and most expert manner without any signal from the drover.

The fatigue that these dogs undergo is very great. One sees them sidle up to their master after each exertion and look at him as if asking for his approbation of what they had done. When I occupied a small farm in Surrey I was in the habit of joining with a friend in the purchase of two hundred Cheviot sheep. The first year we had them the drover who drove them from the north was asked how he had got on: Why, very badly, said the man. For I had a young dog and he did not manage well in keeping the sheep from running up lanes and out of the way places. The next year we had the same number of sheep brought up and by the same man. In answer to our question about his journey he informed us that he had got on very well for his dog had recollected all the turnings of the road which the sheep had passed the previous year and kept them straight the whole of the way."

We learn from this article that the drover's dog had to have some experience of numerous routes before he was accomplished at his work which is why most drovers would have worked a new dog alongside a more experienced animal. This drover's dog demonstrates a high level of intelligence as he was able to recall, a whole year later, a route travelled only once. The writer of the previous excerpt was a shepherd and it is interesting to note that, when he refers to the drover's dog at work, he does not describe it as rough and fierce in nature but states how gentle it was in moving the sheep, causing them no disturbance whatsoever.

In more recent times, the Welsh sheepdog was a popular drover's dog, being used to drive sheep, cattle and even geese, as the Welsh sheepdog is a skilled worker and knows how to control sheep without crowding them.

Drovers and Highwaymen

I have already mentioned that highwaymen were a danger that drovers had to face because of the large sums of money which they frequently carried. To compound the problem, drovers also acted as government agents, bringing ship money to London which had been gathered on behalf of Charles I to pay for his fleet.

Many highwaymen knew that drovers were carrying great wealth about their person and so they obviously targeted them, which generally meant holding them up at the point of a pistol in the outlying areas of London such as Epping or Uxbridge. These highwaymen, despite the romantic tales, were bloody, callous murderers who would kill for a sixpence.

The most notorious highwayman in the early part of the eighteenth century was Dick Turpin and his partner Tom King, with their gang known as the Essex Gang. Dick Turpin had been a butcher in Essex so knew all the drove roads to Barnet Fair and the Essex grazing lands. This knowledge helped him to plan attacks on drovers just where they would least expect it. The drovers would not give in without a fight but, outnumbered by murderous highwaymen, they were often deprived of the money entrusted to them. After selling the flock or herd, the drover was carrying even greater sums of money than on his way to London and, if he lost it to robbers, it was losing money belonging to the farmers and squires who trusted him. Such a loss would completely ruin a drover's reputation and he would no longer be able to find work in that field.

However, on the return journey from market, a drover was no longer restricted to droving roads and could use his extensive knowledge of the country and its highways to thread a route back in an unpredictable manner so as to evade the highwaymen.

Drover's Pay

Drovers made comfortable fortunes for themselves which, it has to be said, they rightly deserved, as their work was not only extremely physically demanding but also very dangerous. It is therefore not surprising that once they secured their deserved fortune, they abandoned the droving way of life. This is one way in which they differed greatly from the shepherd, as the shepherd follows his calling for life. The drover did not see his way of life as a calling, but as a business: the haulier of yesteryear.

Once the drover had amassed a sufficient fortune to set himself up for life, being a man of enterprise he usually turned his attentions to other pursuits. Thomas Williams, for example, opened a bookshop and printing business; Dyfydd Jones became famous as a hymn writer and translator; and

Huw Morus became one of the foremost bards of the late seventeenth century. Huw Morus was known for his poems and also for his charity as the wealth he had earned on the road as a drover enabled him to provide for others. The activities of this small selection of former drovers suggests that they were far from stupid men; often they were men of great depth and some education.

The Corgi

From the fifteenth to the eighteenth century there was a great trade in cattle between England and Wales and the dog that aided the drovers in the movement of the cattle over the hundreds of miles involved was a breed of dog which is still known today.

The Corgi is an agile dog of great stamina and courage who controlled the cattle by nipping at their heels, his speed of movement being so great that, when the cattle kicked out in response to the nip, the dog could dodge the blow and avoid injury. The little dogs had a great deal to do on the long journey from Wales to London. For example, the cattle had to be grazed along the roadside so that they did not lose condition on the long journey or their price would fall. It was the dogs' responsibility to ensure that, whilst the cattle grazed, none was lost: no easy task when the herd could number up to five hundred. Whenever a stagecoach came along, the dogs had to respond rapidly and move the herd to one side so that the coach could pass unhindered. This had to be done without causing a stampede which meant handling them firmly but not pushing too hard and so, just like the larger dogs used for herding sheep, the Corgi had to know exactly how much pressure was acceptable. It was a remarkable facet of the Corgi that it did not have to be trained to work with cattle; it just knew instinctively what to do.

Above and below: The Welsh Corgi, the powerful little dog used by Welsh drovers to drive large herds of cattle to London.

These little Welsh dogs not only drove cattle, they loved to go hunting with their masters whenever the opportunity arose. Records show that a number of them were also trained by shepherds to work with flocks of sheep, but although they were apparently accomplished at the task, they could not match the sheepdog breeds in this field.

Despite their diminutive stature, the Corgis, working in small packs, were always ready to attack any highwayman with the greatest ferocity. This led to many corgis being badly injured or even killed as they fought to protect their masters but they often bought enough time for the drover to raise his own pistol in defence. The corgi's devotion to his master gives rise to a courage that far exceeds the dog's size.

Today many people wish to make their fortune quickly but the drovers of old sought their fortunes with courage, hard work and a great strength of spirit – matched in equal measure by their partner, the drover's dog.

CHAPTER ELEVEN

Sheepdogs in Church

Shepherds attended church every Sunday, and since their dogs went everywhere with them, they felt that it was perfectly natural for them to go to church as well. Consequently, on a Sunday morning, there could be dozens of sheepdogs in the rural congregation which, not surprisingly, had an effect on the way that the service was delivered as related in *Notes And Queries (1876)*:

An Edinburgh minister standing in for the regular minister was performing service one Sunday in a remote country Kirk where dogs formed no inconsiderable part of the congregation. It is the custom of the Scotch Kirk for the assembled worshippers to stand while the blessing is pronounced. When the minister however rose for the purpose at the end of the service he perceived to his surprise that his hearers all remained seated. He looked around for some little time with an expectant eye but no one moved. At last the clerk, with the view of relieving the honest gentleman's confusion, turned up his head from his desk below and bawled out "Say on, sir, it's just to cheat the dogs." It had been found that the dogs, imagining the service to be concluded when the congregation stood up at this crisis always prepared for their own departure and disturbed the solemnity of the occasion by various canine noises and shufflings; they had therefore to be circumvented by the people keeping their seats while the benediction was given.

It is a mark of how highly the community viewed the shepherd that they made such allowances for their dogs and also gives some insight into how the shepherd thought as he saw no disrespect in attending church with a dog by his

The dog-noper. Nope in northern dialect means to knock on the head.

side. He and his dog were so accustomed to being constantly together that it was unthinkable to leave him behind.

The attendance at church of the shepherd's dogs was also a feature of rural life in Ireland, as shown in the following account written by the Rev. J.E. Vaux in 1902:

About twenty years ago I was in Connemara salmon fishing. The first Sunday the landlord of the hotel where I was staying kindly offered me a seat in his car to convey me to chapel on the bog three or four miles off for the midday Mass. I gladly accepted the lift. The chapel was of the most primitive kind. The floor was but of beaten clay. When I entered, the altar rail was closely packed with worshippers who I presume were all shepherds. There was only one pew which belonged to the 'quality' i.e the landlord and his family. I preferred to kneel alongside my attendant ghillie (to use a Scotch term) who was there.

There were a dozen dogs at least in the chapel, several of them sitting behind their masters who were kneeling at the altar rail. One of these sheepdogs attracted my attention. He sat most quietly through the earlier portion of the service. As soon as the creed had been recited and the celebrant turned round to deliver the sermon, the dog looked up as much as to say, 'Oh, sermon time, all right,' and having, dog fashion, walked round three times curled himself up for a comfortable sleep. The sermon, which did not last more than ten minutes, being over, the dog woke up and sat on his tail behind his shepherd master until the service was over. There was something so deliciously human about this that I have never forgotten it. I have described the incident exactly as it happened without the slightest exaggeration.

I wonder if Rev. Vaux remembered the sermon as well as he remembered the shepherd's dog?

The Sociable Sheepdog

It is a feature of the sheepdog that he is happy to simply be near his master and does not need to be the centre of attention.

On many occasions, I have been working outside in rain or snow and my Collies will be curled up close by rather than be left kennelled in the warm and dry. They ask only

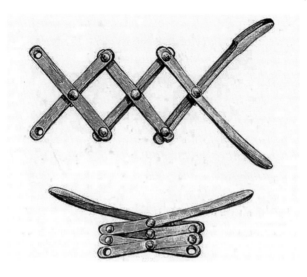

The type of dog tongs used to remove fighting dogs from churches.

to be close by, so I allow them to accompany me whenever possible.

Of course, having large numbers of dogs in church could, on occasion, lead to problems and, indeed, fights: something that sheepdogs seem to rather enjoy. The task of keeping an eye on the dogs and breaking up any fights fell to the churchwarden, who would often get nipped for his trouble.

In Welsh rural churches there must have been frequent fights for they designed dog tongs to save the warden's hands from a nasty bite. It must be remembered that this was in the days before antibiotics and an infection, now easily treatable, could prove life-threatening. Herbalists knew that honey could help inhibit bacterial growth and keep a wound clean but a dog bite was a serious matter and, with many dogs in the congregation, the purchase of dog tongs was justified.

These expanding tongs were used to grasp the trouble-maker by the neck or the leg so that he could be removed from the service. There are records of these tongs being used in Wales and the Welsh borders but they do not appear to have been used in the Scottish Highlands: maybe the Scottish sheepdogs were just better behaved!

In some of the grander churches in England, the Isle of Man and Wales, sheepdogs were not allowed inside the building and beadles were appointed to ensure that the dogs stayed outside. They were known as dognopers and received a salary for this duty. It appears that dognopers were frequently also gravediggers, making much of their living performing the routine tasks of the busy churchyard. As a dognoper could be managing fifty or more dogs at a larger church, he might also have used a small whip by way of a deterrent.

CHAPTER TWELVE

Sheep Stealers
and their Dogs

Written accounts indicate that the shepherd of old was a God-fearing man but there were, of course, some rare exceptions. The most notorious of these were the sheep stealers; shepherds who used their craft in a deeply dishonest manner, sneaking about the hills at night to deprive other shepherds of their sheep. Great wealth could be acquired by the organized thief but, when caught, the sheep stealer often came up with some wild excuses to try and escape responsibility for his crime as the punishment was death by hanging.

One young man, caught in the possession of another man's sheep, actually tried to shift the blame for the theft onto his dog who, though an accomplice, had simply done as he was told. Dogs may possess great levels of intelligence but, of course, they cannot assess the moral integrity of an undertaking. For example, during World War II, German shepherds (Alsatian dogs) were used in the concentration camps to ensure that the Jewish prisoners did not escape. The Nazis who handled these dogs were without doubt men of extreme evil for they had the power to make a moral judgement and choose their actions but the dogs simply did as they were bid. Dogs have the power to reason to a degree, but it is down to man to see that the dog's actions are kept within the bounds of the law.

The Ettrick Shepherd (James Hogg) whom I have already quoted on the nature of the shepherd and his dogs, records the story of the young sheep stealer who tried to blame his dog for his crimes:

One young man, who was, I believe, overtaken by justice for his first offence, stated that after he had stolen the sheep by moonlight selecting his number from the flock of a former master he took them out and set away with them toward Edinburgh. But before he had got them quite off the farm his conscience smote him, as he said, and he quitted the sheep, letting them go again to the hill. He called his dog off them and mounting his pony he rode away. At that time, he said, his dog was capering and playing around him as if glad of having got free of a troublesome business; and he regarded him no more till after having rode about three miles he thought again and again that he heard something coming up behind him.

Halting at length to ascertain what it was, in a few minutes there comes his dog with the stolen animals, driving them at a furious rate to keep up with his master. The sheep were all smoking and hanging out their tongues and their guide was as fully as warm as they. The young man was now exceedingly troubled for the sheep having been brought so far from home he dreaded that there would be a pursuit and he could not get them home again before day. Resolving at all events to keep his hands clear of them he corrected his dog in great wrath, left the sheep once more and taking the collie with him rode off a second time.

He had not ridden above a mile till he perceived that his assistant had again given him the slip and suspecting for what purpose he was terribly alarmed as well as chagrined, for daylight now approached and he durst not make a noise calling his dog for fear of alarming the neighbourhood in a place where they were well known. He resolved therefore to abandon the animal to himself and take a road across the country, which he was sure the other did not know and could not follow. He took the road, for being on horseback he could not get across the enclosed fields. He at length came to a gate, which he shut behind him and went about half a mile farther by a zigzag course to a farmhouse where both his sister and sweetheart lived and at that place he remained until after breakfast time.

The people of this house were all examined at the trial and no one had either seen the sheep or heard them mentioned save one man who came up to the sheep thief as he was standing at the stable door and told him that his dog had the sheep safe enough down at the Crooked Yett so he need not hurry himself. He answered that the sheep were young Mr Thomson's who had left them to his charge as

The sheep stealer plied his dishonest craft as darkness cloaked the land.

he was in search of a man to drive them, which made him come off the road. After this discovery; it was impossible for the poor fellow to get quit of them so he went down and took possession of the stolen drove once more, carried them on and disposed of them and finally the transaction cost him his life.

It is quite strange that this young shepherd should lose his nerve at the point at which the flock is gathered and he is about to make off with them. Possibly a sudden fear for his neck prompted the about-turn but, for some reason, his dog did not believe him. It is most strange that the dog went and re-gathered the sheep for, in the course of its normal work, the dog would have been used to gathering sheep that were held for a short time and then released back to the hill.

This sheepdog pursued his master with the sheep even after he had been heavily chastised for his work and yet still the dog did not swerve from its task. The young shepherd had intended to steal the sheep and knew which sheep he would take, the route he would use and their destination, all of which the dog seemed to understand and would not be convinced that his master's plans had changed. This dog, loyal and determined to fulfil what he perceived to be his master's request, may have cost the shepherd his life for, once the sheep were at the nearby inn and it became apparent that there was no pursuit, the young shepherd did not return the sheep, took them to Edinburgh and sold them. His intent could not be denied and hanging was inevitable.

Hanging as a punishment for sheep stealing was practised for hundreds of years until around 1825. It is not known whether shepherds considered the punishment a fitting one; hanging was, after all, a common form of punishment at that time for all kinds of theft. James Hogg, the Ettrick Shepherd, in his writing refers to the hanging of sheep stealers as sad but does not condemn the punishment.

The law has moved on a great deal since those days

and in 1937 a man found guilty of stealing 57 sheep was sentenced to nine months in prison.

Not all sheep stealers were incompetent like the young shepherd hanged after committing his first crime and some thieves were highly organized and very successful, making vast sums of money from their crimes.

★★★★★

One of the most successful sheep-stealing gangs comprised a farmer by the name of Alexander Murdison and his shepherd John Millar who operated in the Scottish Border country around 1760. Their great success was put down to the shepherd's sagacious dog that went by the name of Yarrow. During daylight, shepherd Millar would point out to Yarrow the sheep he wanted the dog to steal that night and, when darkness fell, the dog would be sent on its dishonest mission.

Shepherd Millar would wait some distance away so that if the dog was, by some chance, spotted stealing, the dog alone would take the blame. However, in all the years that he stole sheep, the sly dog never was spotted. When Yarrow brought the sheep to shepherd Millar, the two would make their way over the high ground towards Murdison's farm.

If they had stolen from a good distance away and daylight came before there was chance to get back to the farm, shepherd Millar would drop into the valley below to make sure he was seen by his fellow shepherds, whilst Yarrow continued along the high ground, faithfully taking the sheep back to the farm.

They were then hidden in an old square tower till their brands and ear marks could be doctored by the thieves. During this work, Yarrow was stationed outside the tower so if anybody approached he would alert his master and Murdison within, to stop their illegal work and hide all evidence quickly so as to avoid discovery. The sheep, once re-marked, were then turned out among Murdison's own flock and taken to market as normal by an unsuspecting drover who had no part in the crime.

The illegal industry that Murdison and his shepherd Millar were running was brought to an end when a ewe, whose markings had been doctored, managed to return to the hill were she was born. The shepherd on that farm, carrying out a flock inspection, suddenly spotted the ewe that he had missed for several months. As he examined her, the shepherd discovered that her markings had been changed into the markings of Murdison. He reported the matter to his master who promptly went to the police.

When Murdison and his shepherd were arrested, three hundred and thirty stolen sheep were discovered on his farm. They were tried in Edinburgh at the High Court in front of no less than six High Court judges, giving an indication of how seriously the crime was viewed. Murdison and Millar were defended by eight noted lawyers, a legal team that must have cost a fortune to secure, which would suggest that they had vast sums of money at their disposal and also that they were desperate to cheat the hangman's noose.

The following account from the *Edinburgh Advertiser* dated January 12th 1773 reports the outcome of the case:

The trial of Murdison and Millar for sheep stealing mentioned in our last continued from 8 o'clock on Friday morning till 5 o'clock on Sunday morning. The examination of the witnesses lasted till five o clock on Saturday night when the Lord Advocate summed up the evidence for the Crown as did Mr Crosbie and Mr Rae, very ably, for the prisoners. The jury inclosed at 11, and did not dismiss till 5 o'clock next morning and yesterday they returned the following verdict: That by a great plurality of voices find the following articles of the indictment proven against the said panel, Alexander Murdison, viz. In so far as regards 8 ewes, of 11 ewes and the tup hogg, the property of William Gibson, tenant in Newby, in the county of Peebles and one ewe, the property of James Hislop, herd to the said William Gibson, which were found on the farm of Ormiston, alias Wormiston; also, in regard to 20 ewes, part of 21 ewes, the property of Thomas Gibson, tenant in Grieston in the county afore-said, found on the panels farm aforesaid; and all in one voice find the following articles of the indictment proven against the said Alexander Murdison, viz, in so far as regards the 15 hoggs, the property of Robert Horseburgh, tenant in Colquhair, in the county aforesaid, and 13 hoggs, the property of the above mentioned William Gibson, sold by the said Alexander Murdison to John Berham, tenant in Westhope in the county of Haddington, and found in the said farm of Westhope, as also, in so far as regards the 16 ewes and 4 hoggs, the property of Walter Simpson, tenant in Easter Dawick in the county of Peebles and found on the farm of the said panel; and in one voice find the indictment proven against John Millar, the other panel, in so far as regards the 10 ewes and lambs, the property of George Cranston Esq, of Dewar and 11 ewes and lambs, the property of David Tweedie, tenant in Ladyside in the county of Edinburgh.

Being found guilty of one charge would have been sufficient to send the men to the gallows; the fact that so many charges were placed against the men demonstrates the determination of the court to bring them to book for serious theft that had occurred in numerous counties and over many years, adding up to hundreds and hundreds of sheep. The *Edinburgh Advertiser* for 26th March 1773 records the final chapter in this sorry tale:

On Wednesday Alexander Murdison and John Millar, for sheep stealing and John Watson for house-breaking were executed in the Grassmarket, agreeable to their sentence. They appeared penitent and behaved as became persons in their unhappy situation.

Nothing much is known about what happened to Yarrow, Millar's very able sheep-stealing dog.

CHAPTER THIRTEEN

The Early Days of Shepherding in Australia

IN THE EARLY DAYS of shepherding in Australia, large numbers of shepherds from Scotland, Ireland and Wales travelled to that distant land, encountering Aborigines, extreme temperatures, snakes and dingos. These were all unknown to the shepherd but they had to adapt quickly. A new breed of sheepdog was developed and new methods of shepherding evolved so that, in spite of the harshness of the land and climate, great fortunes were made from the sale of Merino wool.

In Great Britain, the shepherd had to deal with very few predators: in some areas, the Golden Eagle and, of course, the fox, but both preyed upon lambs rather than full-grown sheep. In this new country, their main predator was much more fearsome and cunning and could kill hundreds of sheep in a single night. The dingo could cause tremendous losses to a flock and became the shepherd's principal enemy. Dingos can be found as lone animals, in pairs or, in the worse case, hunting in small packs.

Before fencing was used, they would sneak up on a flock of sheep and drive it away with the skill of a Border Collie, taking them into a blind gully. One or two would then guard the entrance, whilst other members of the pack would rush into the flock, ripping at the throats of the terrified and defenceless sheep with their powerful jaws. For the shepherd who tended his valuable flock with such care and devotion, the discovery of so many of his charges slaughtered in this way must have been horrific and it is not surprising that he declared war on the dingo, killing him by whatever means he could.

The only way to cover the vast distances in this new country was on horseback but this was nothing new as the shepherds of the Scottish Highlands and the Welsh hills had always been horsemen. It is said that one of the ways they would dispatch dingos was to chase them on horseback and, as they neared the fleeing dingo, the shepherd would nimbly reach down, remove his stirrup leather and land the dingo a single fatal blow on the back of the head with the stirrup iron.

Dingos were also shot, trapped and poisoned with strychnine. This led to a problem as it was not uncommon for a sheepdog to pick up the bait left for a dingo and be poisoned: so it became necessary to train sheepdogs to ignore all forms of bait. Frank Townend Barton M.R.C.V.S wrote the following about strychnine in 1903 when the poison was widely used in this country to destroy moles and foxes.

"Strychnine poisoning appears almost immediately after the animal has consumed this agent, even in an infinitessimal quantity. It is denoted by a series of rapid titanic convulsions, or muscular spasms, which completely distort the body and produce the most agonising features."

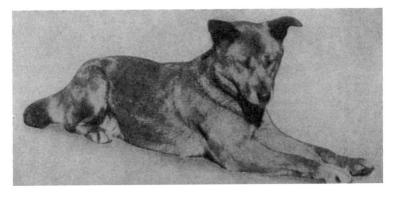

The savage and sagacious Dingo.

In fact, poisoning by this agent is extremely cruel and anyone giving it deliberately to a dog should be punished accordingly. The excessive level of destruction caused by the ruthless dingo, however, surely prompted the shepherd to use this most devastating poison, as the dingo was not an easy animal to hunt with a rifle and was extremely cautious around traps.

Some shepherds, however, did recognize some value in the dingo in the respect that, being a member of the dog family, it could be crossed with a sheepdog. The sheepdogs taken to Australia by the pioneering shepherds had been bred to work in the cold and wet of the hills and mountains, but in this hot and arid land they were soon overcome by the strong sun. A breed of dog was required that could cope with the specific needs of shepherding in Australia; that is, working with exceptionally large flocks, running to thousands, in extreme heat and over very long distances.

The root-stock of this new breed was some kind of smooth-coated Collie imported from Scotland, which, after several breedings, became acclimatized to the conditions.

The Kelpie

One of the pups thrown was a black and tan bitch named Kelpie: she won the first sheepdog trial ever held in Australia. The pups she bore were called Kelpie's pups and it was not long before Kelpie became the name for this breed of dog. Its ability to work tirelessly all day long with no amount of sun being too much, meant the breed spread rapidly right across Australia. With one of these dogs, the shepherd (who soon became known in Australia as a stockman) could muster a flock of sheep, (which was known in Australia as a mob) maybe thousands in number and spread over thousands of acres, in just one day. The same job done by a crew of men mounted on horseback without such a dog would take up to a week.

The original stock from which the Kelpie sprang had no dingo in its breeding but it is believed that the Kelpie of today has some dingo blood to give it that strength and endurance. In spite of this, the Kelpie is a very sensitive dog and cannot tolerate rough handling. Use harsh words on him and he completely loses his composure; strike him and you ruin him forever.

The Kelpie works his sheep from a distance, never coming much closer than a hundred yards and driving them with a great evenness of pace. This is important as the sheep are often moved from one paddock to another to seek out fresh grazing and, if they were pushed hard, their condition would suffer. The Kelpie will bring the sheep as far as the yard but, once inside, he is of very little use as he does not like close proximity with the sheep, and so for close work the

The classic sheep of Australia: the heavily-fleeced Merino.

first cousin of the Kelpie is called upon; a much bolder dog called the Barb.

If, for example, the sheep cause a bottleneck, refusing to go through a paddock gate, the Barb does not waste time barking at the back of the jammed-up flock but suddenly springs onto the backs of the sheep, runs across them to the front of the flock where the problem lies and, snapping and barking, he soon has the blockage moving. The job of controlling very large flocks of up to twenty thousand sheep at close quarters is a very demanding one and the Barb is more than willing to dive in and use his teeth on an offending sheep that thinks it can overcome the will of the dog.

The distinction between the Kelpie and the Barb has diminished as all Australian sheepdogs are now termed Kelpies, but, from the early 1800s to as late as the 1940s, there were certainly two distinct, though closely related, breeds. It is great testament to the dog-breeding skills and knowledge of the Scottish shepherds that they could go to such an alien environment and, within the space of a few decades, develop a dog so well-suited to the rigours of working under the hot Australian sun.

The shepherds themselves also adapted quickly to the new country, becoming skilled bushmen, only bettered in bushcraft by the native Aborigine. These tough country folk had such a deep understanding of nature that they could readily adjust to the vastly different working environment.

Finally, to give you an idea of how very tough the Kelpie is, I shall tell the story of Coil. Coil was at a sheepdog trial in Sydney which was run over several days. On the first day, he had been awarded the full one hundred points for his sterling performance on the course. However, on his way home that evening, there was an accident and Coil suffered a broken leg. His owner made a splint for the poor dog using sheet cork, which would have provided an ideal light but stable splint. The following day, despite the broken leg, Coil completed the final course in six minutes and twelve seconds and again gained the maximum one hundred points for his performance.

An Australian sheepdog demonstrates the amazing ability of that breed to run across the backs of corralled sheep.

CHAPTER FOURTEEN

Shepherding in Other Parts of the World

Shepherd dogs have been used in nearly every part of the world: in Iran and Turkey, right across Europe, in India, which at that time encompassed Pakistan, in China, in Africa and, of course, in America. There were and, in fact, still are sheepdogs even in the arctic such as the Icelandic sheepdog and the Buhund of Norway. I shall restrict my comments here to the huge dogs used in the highlands of the European countries such as the Pyrenees, dividing Spain and France, and the Alps dividing Italy and Switzerland.

In these regions, the dogs used by shepherds were of a huge, powerful and fierce nature, as the remoteness of the mountains meant that groups of bandits could steal, rape and murder anyone who had not the power to stand against them. No place was considered sacred by these evil men as even the monastery of St Bernard, a hospice located on a treacherous trading route between Italy and Switzerland high in the Swiss Alps, was attacked on a cold day in 1787. It is beyond doubt that the hospice would have been ransacked and all the Brothers killed without mercy had it not been for a pack of 15 of the most fearsome St Bernard dogs who attacked the heavily armed bandits, driving them, torn and bloody, back into the hills.

Flocks of sheep and farms in the mountain regions were at risk from such attacks by bloodthirsty and lawless men, which is why every farm had its own pack of dogs and every flock was guarded by dogs such as the Pyrenean mountain dog, the Liptok and the large Swiss mountain dogs which were used to guard both sheep and cattle. The Pyrenean

The Portuguese sheepdog from the Estrela mountain range. This dog is 26 inches at the shoulder and weighs 100lbs.

The Romanian sheepdog of the Transylvanian uplands. This dog is 26 inches at the shoulder and weighs 110lbs.

would walk ahead of the sheep going out to pasture and, as the sheep settled down to grazing, the giant dogs would take up position on some high point and keep a constant vigil. If any man or wild animal came close to their charges, they would be savagely repelled.

In the mountains, before the 1800s, the sheep were at risk of attack from many wild creatures such as bear, lynx and of course packs of wolves. This is another reason why the mountain shepherd dogs of Europe had to be so big and to work in packs, as even a pack of wolves or a bear will think twice before tackling a pack of mountain sheepdogs. The Pyrenean, for example, weighs a hefty 115lbs and stands up to 32 inches at the shoulder. The weight of the European wolf is roughly 100lbs and it stands between 27 and 30 inches at the shoulder, which means that the European mountain sheepdogs are more than able to tackle him. The wolf has a 30 percent larger brain than the dog and he soon deduces that it is not worth tangling with a pack of sheepdogs for, even if the pack of wolves is larger, it will suffer injuries or losses that are not worth risking unless the wolves are starving. Even the European bear weighing 300kg will not tackle a pack of sheepdogs for, as he tackles one dog, the others could inflict a serious injury: so the pack of sheepdogs are a most effective method of protecting sheep, cattle and farmsteads.

In Switzerland, Romania and other parts of Europe, the size of the mountain sheepdog is often put to good use by harnessing the dogs to small carts to take produce from the farm to local markets or hitching them up to harness and chains to haul logs felled for firewood.

During the winter months, when the mountains are heavily snowed-up, the stock is kept in barns where it is hay-fed and the shepherd is, of course, then at home with his family. As the warmer weather comes and the snow recedes, the sheep are moved onto the lower slopes to graze on the low

The Liptok sheepdog of the kind that would guard a fold of sheep in the Tatra mountains.

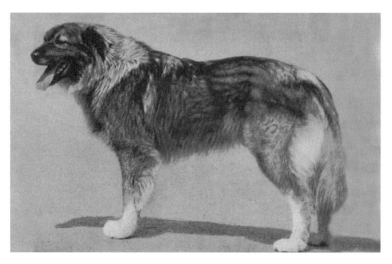

The Illyrian sheepdog, a Croat dog from the northern ranges of the Illyrian mountains. This dog is 23 inches at the shoulder and weighs 60lbs.

A pair of Swiss mountain dogs hauling a cart loaded with wool sacks.

mountain pasture and the shepherd and his flock and pack of dogs remain there for the following five to six months, living in a small mountain hut till the snow returns. Life would be very isolated, with only the occasional visit back to the farm below, when the shepherd often left the flock under the charge of the dogs with perhaps one of the pack returning to the farm with its master to keep him company.

Life on the mountain pasture is therefore lonely for the shepherd unless he has a son with him. Some of the time on the mountain is spent hunting for chamois, a goat-like antelope of the mountains of Europe, which would provide useful skins and cured meat to tide the shepherd's family through the tough winter months.

Whilst watching over the flock, shepherds throughout the world would make cloaks from sheepskin for themselves

174

The German shepherd dog has found many new roles in the modern world. Above, for example, he works for the R.A.F police. Below: And here he is being trained to be winched from a helicopter for mountain rescue operations.

and their family to keep them warm against the coldest winter and many shepherds could also knit, making socks and other garments. This was particularly the case amongst British shepherds for whom knitting, far from being considered a female preserve, was a skill considered an essential requirement for the rural dweller who made most of their own clothing. Woodcarving and fine stitchwork were also practised among the mountain shepherds.

When not hunting or making things, shepherds would often entertain themselves by playing a small flute that would have been fashioned from a suitable stick and the mountain dogs apparently enjoyed the music. To move the sheep, the big dogs would bark and if that did not work, they would nip them gently on the neck. The dogs would often be at some distance from the shepherd and were commanded by the use of a long horn or blasts on the shepherd's flute, which is similar to the dog whistle used by shepherds in this country.

The constant preparation of the mountain shepherd for the forthcoming winter, using everything in his immediate environment to help him to survive is a way of life that has very much died out. People today rely heavily on others for the manufacture and production of food and clothing but the early shepherds had to make all that they needed to live comfortably themselves; a practical way of life, especially in austere times.

Nowadays, Alpine sheepdogs have all but lost their occupation, due to the near extinction of the bigger european predators and the fact that even the remotest parts of the mountains are now law-abiding. However, one of the large sheepdogs which was used to guard flocks and farmsteads in Germany and which can trace its roots back as far as the seventh century has found many new roles in a changing world; that dog is, of course, none other than the German sheepdog, the Alsatian.

CHAPTER FIFTEEN

Shepherd Arts, Pastimes, Implements and Folklore

Apart from being able to read and write and often deeply religious, shepherds were fit and athletic as this piece written in 1590 by Spenser reveals:

In wrestling, nimble and in running, swift;
In shooting, steddy and in swimming strong;
Well made to strike, to throw, to leap, to lift,
And all the sports that shepherds are emong.

This description of the shepherd's abilities depicts him as someone who would have excelled at Highland games or wrestling matches at local fairs. Another quotation from the sixteenth century that appeared in Barclay's *Eclogues* gives a similar depiction but this time also mentions the shepherd's musical interests.

I can dance the raye, I can both pipe and sing,
If I were mery; I can both hurle and sling;
I runne, I wrestle, I can well throwe the barre,
No shepherd throweth the axeltree so farre;
If I were mery, I could well leape and spring;
I were a man mete to serve a prince or king.

An axletree is the bar around which a wagon wheel revolves. The writer mentions the shepherd's ability to sling, or his skill with a sling shot, like that used by David in the Bible to slay Goliath. In 1801, Joseph Strutt wrote

A shepherd sporting a crook made from an old gun barrel and a less-than-straight stick (c.1880).

the following interesting article about this ancient aspect of shepherd life:

The art of slinging, or casting of stones with a sling, is of high antiquity, and probably antecedent to that of archery, though not so generally known nor so generally practised. It was, perhaps, an instrument much used by the shepherds in ancient times, to protect their flocks from the attacks of ferocious animals; if so, we shall not wonder that David, who kept his father's sheep, was so expert in the management of this weapon.

I remember in my youth to have seen several persons expert in slinging of stones, which they performed with thongs of leather, or wanting those, with garters, and sometimes they used a stick of ash or hazel, a yard or better in length, and about an inch in diameter; it was split at the top so as to make an opening wide enough to receive a stone, which was confined by the reaction of the stick on both sides, but not strong enough to resist the impulse of the slinger.

It required much practice to handle this instrument with any degree of certainty, for if the stone in the act of throwing quitted the sling either sooner or later than it ought to do, the desired effect was sure to fail. Those who could use it properly cast stones to a considerable distance and with much precision. In the present day (1800) the use of these engines seems to be totally discontinued.

Mention has been made of the shepherd's musical ability with the pipe and he would have learnt this skill as a lad along with how to make his own wooden pipe from a suitable wood such as apple, which provides a mellow tone. Richard Jefferies wrote in 1880 about the piping of a shepherd boy.

A shepherd lad will sit under the trees and as you pass along the track comes the mellow note of his wooden whistle from which poor instrument he draws a sweet sound. There is no tune, no recognizable melody; he plays from his heart and to himself. In a room doubtless

The shepherd and his wife busy at lambing time.

it would seem harsh and discordant but there the player unseen, his simple notes harmonize with the open plain, the looming hills, the ruddy sunset as if striving to express the feelings these call forth.

It is a shame that the shepherds' music is no longer a part of the rural scene. It is telling that the shepherds did not play recognized tunes but found the music within themselves, a richness and joy in their souls expressed in the wild captivating music of the pipe.

A far more practical shepherding instrument is the shepherd's crook, shown in paintings from medieval times as being an elegant, straight, fine stick. The reality was far from the case, it being a much coarser tool created from whatever the shepherd had to hand, as explained by Richard Jefferies, the late-Victorian natural history writer, in 1887.

The shepherd was very ready and pleased to show his crook, which however was not symmetrical in shape as those which are represented upon canvas. Nor was the handle straight; it was a rough stick, the first evidently that had come to hand. As there were no hedges or copses near his sheep walks he had to be content with this bent wand till he could get a better. The iron crook itself, he said, was made by a blacksmith in a village below.

A good crook was often made from the barrel of an old single barrel gun which was past its best and which the shepherd had replaced by a better one. About a foot of the barrel being sawn off at the muzzle end there was a tube at once to fit the staff into, while the crook was formed by hammering the tough metal into a curve upon the anvil. So the gun, the very symbol of destruction was beaten into a pastoral crook, the implement and emblem of peace.

Another of the shepherd's implements was the shepherd's bottle which was, in fact, a small wooden cask, as pictured on page 136. The bottle is attached to the pole over the young drover's shoulder. It is an implement of great antiquity as indicated by a few lines from *The Shepherd And His Wife* (1590):

A bottle full of country whig
By the shepherd's side did lig

Lig is old English for lie. A.L.J. Gosset can tell us more about the shepherd's bottle:

The little kegs or wooden barrels in which the shepherds used to carry their cold thin drink are still remembered as bottles. The contents were generally innocent enough. It might be herb beer made from the small dandelion, the burnet, tops of nettles, ginger, sugar and yeast; or home brewed beer hops, sugar and ginger, some added a little malt. Others preferred to drink cider. Many of the old poets write of whig, which was whey or buttermilk. In the Ancient Drama it is thus described; from the whey of milk; after the cheese curd has been separated from the whey by an acid mixture it is called whig and drunk by the poor classes as beer.

In previous centuries, people did not drink water because it was unsafe, especially in areas of high population, cholera being a real and present danger. Beers and ciders were

A shepherd lad and his affectionate dog watching over the flock.

rendered safe by the process of fermentation and so were drunk as a healthier alternative to water.

A major influence on the shepherd's life, and thus a great part of their folk-lore, was the weather. When the sheep begin to go up the mountains, the shepherd says it will be fine weather but when they come down the hill to take shelter on the lower ground, it does not matter how fine the weather may look, a storm is on the way.

Another shepherds' saying is that March borrows the first few days from April because they are of a stormy nature. In William Hone's *Every-Day Book* of 1826 it tells how, before a storm comes, the sheep assemble at one corner of a field, turning their backs to the wind. Old sheep are said to eat greedily before a bad storm and sparingly before a thaw.

Of course, one of the most common shepherd sayings is "red sky at night, shepherd's delight, red sky in the morning, shepherd's warning." I suppose it is not at all surprising that shepherds used their sheep for a daily weather forecast, for sheep seem to have the ability to detect a storm long before it grips the country.

In this, as in many other matters, the shepherd learned to listen, watch and trust what the animals told him, without speaking a single word.

Brief Glossary of Shepherding Terms

Barren or **Geld** – A ewe that has failed to come into lamb after being covered by the ram.

Broken Mouthed – An old sheep with lose or missing teeth.

Cast – A sheep that is stuck on its back unable to get back to its feet.

Dagging – The clipping of soiled wool from around the tail.

Ewe – An adult female sheep.

Gimmer – A young female sheep.

Heft – A defined area of ground grazed by a number of sheep usually one or two hundred sheep.

Hirsel – Numerous hefts that make up the ground under a shepherd's charge and the sheep upon them.

Hogg – A young male or female sheep between weaning and its first shearing.

Lamb – The term given to a sheep until it is weaned.

Ram or **Tup** – Both terms for an entire male sheep.

Raddle – A powder to which liquid is added to form a marking paste applied to the chest of a ram so that he marks the backs of the females he covers.

Shearling – A male, female or castrated lamb between its first and second shearing

Wether – A castrated male.

Acknowledgements

Erwyd Howells and his dogs

I would like to offer my special thanks to Erwyd Howells (local historian, Welsh language expert and hill shepherd) for his invaluable assistance in the compilation of this book.

Bibliography

Good Men and True, Erwyd Howells, published 2005,
ISBN 0-9551736-0-4
The life of Welsh hill shepherds in the Aberystwyth area.

The Ettrick Shepherd, Vol. 2, James Hogg; published by Hamilton Adams and Co. 1886.

Sheep Dogs and their Masters, John Herries McCulloch, published by The Moray Press, 1938.

British War Dogs, their training and psychology, E.H Richardson, published by Skeffington and Son.

Working Dogs of the World, Clifford L.B Hubbard, published by Sidgwick & Jackson, 1947.

Shepherds of Britain, A.L.J Gosset, published by Constable, 1911.